The Joyfully Married
Couple's Journal

A Year of Questions to Ignite Fun Conversations and Grow Your Love

Jed Jurchenko

www.CoffeeShopConversations.com

To Jenny
I'm thrilled and blessed to be
on this amazing adventure with you!

Introduction

Welcome to *The Joyfully Married Couple's Journal*. This book contains 365 creative connection questions—one for each day of the year. When I ask couples, "How do you know you are joyfully married?" some common responses include:

- We love spending time together.
- We enjoy the same things.
- We watch movies together.
- We give each other our undivided attention.
- We look across the room and just know what the other person is thinking.
- We talk about everything.
- We are sexually and emotionally attracted to one another.
- We feel in synch.

I asked this question to hundreds of couples, and nearly every answer shares the common theme of connection. Some couples explain what it feels like to be connected, while others share a meaningful connection moment. Many responses are modest, which shows that small gestures can have an immense impact.

Feeling connected to our loved one is powerful because human beings have an innate longing to know and to be known. In Genesis 2:18, God said, "It is not good for the man to be alone. I will make a companion for him who corresponds to him." The very first human beings were God-designed to connect, and this has not changed.

The importance of a strong bond is also confirmed by science. Schizoid Personality Disorder, for example, is a diagnosis found in *The Diagnostic and Statistical Manual of Mental Disorders* or *DSM* for short. Although this diagnosis has an extensive criterion, the summation is that schizoid individuals do not want close relationships, nor do they desire them. According to psychology, when the yearning to bond is absent, something is amiss.

Strong emotional bonds, on the other hand, are highly celebrated. We refer to the intertwining of hearts as "falling in love," and wedding ceremonies are some of the most extravagant parties around. Finding love is so grand that nineteenth-century pastor Peter Marshal called marriage, "the halls of highest human happiness," and this universal marvel is lavishly celebrated throughout the world.

This goal of this journal is to help you and your spouse to fall more deeply in love than ever before by developing a steady connection habit. This journal will help you to incorporate two key components of love—action and intimacy. But before examining exactly how this journal works, let's first take a moment to explore what love is, what love is not, and how action and intimacy can add value to your bond.

Love, Action, and Intimacy

Contrary to popular belief, love is not something we haphazardly fall in and out of. Love is a verb, and like all verbs, love requires action. Just as eyes blink and hearts beat, love knows another person deeply and acts kindly toward them. This is wonderful news because feelings are fickle—they come, they go, and they change over time. But because love is a choice, it can remain steady for a lifetime.

To be fully known and completely accepted is one of the deepest desires of the human heart. Love entails knowing our spouse deeply and cherishing him or her fully—flaws and all. This is what intimacy, or as I prefer to call it, into-me-see, is all about. Intimacy is the ability to peer into our partner's inner world while simultaneously allowing our self to be known. It comes from a mutual sharing of hopes, fears, sorrows, and joys. This can be terrifying because the thought, *Will I still be loved after revealing the true me?* is infinitely present.

Breaking through this barrier takes kindness, curiosity, and a relentless pursuit—which is what this journal will help you to accomplish. Each page contains a single question that invites you to embark on a connection adventure. Some questions are humorous, while others are deep. There are conversation starters with a spiritual focus, inquiries that dive into the past, and questions that encourage you to dream about your future.

Yet the goal is always the same. Each entry will assist you in further exploring your loved one's inner world. Below the daily question, you'll find separate lines for each of you to record your answers. Under these are two additional sections where you can repeat this process for two more years. This allows you to reflect on your growth and turns this journal into a valuable keepsake.

But please know there is no one correct way to use this book. The decision to journal for one year or three, to write your answers down, talk about them, or to do both is entirely up to you. As long as you and your spouse are drawing closer together, you are doing things right!

The Power of Love

You are probably already aware of the astonishing power of love—after all, you are reading this book. Nevertheless, here are three important reminders of the value of love. These facts can serve as motivation for pressing forward on challenging days.

First, a kind, caring relationship with our spouse makes life's bright moments brighter. Love provides our brain with a dose of oxytocin—a mood-boosting neuropeptide, also known as the cuddle hormone. This adds an extra layer of joy to everyday life. Second, love keeps us healthier by strengthening our immune system. This decreases our susceptibility to common viruses like the cold and flu. And because love reduces stress, it also provides added protection against mental illness and heart attacks. Finally, love is so powerful that one study shows it actually causes physical pain to hurt less.[1]

These truths not only provide excellent motivation for staying connected, but they also prove something the best fairytales have known all along. Loving couples are among the happiest people on earth. Yet most fairytales have one major flaw. That final line about couples living happily ever after—this is utter nonsense.

After the wedding, there are still plenty of dragons to slay, challenges to face, and adventures to be had. If fairytales wanted to portray a more accurate view of marriage, they would write something like this instead.

After the prince rescued his true love, the town gathered to celebrate their marriage. The couple recited their vows, and there was an extravagant feast. Then, the handsome prince and beautiful princess mounted their steed and rode into the sunset—and this was when the real adventure began...

Marriage is only the beginning of a much grander adventure. Unlike other relationship books, this journal is not about resolving relationship problems but instead focuses on enjoying the adventure. It contains questions from a number of my bestselling books—including *131 Creative Conversations for Couples*, *131 Engaging Conversations for Couples*, and *131 Necessary Conversations Before Marriage*—as well as some entirely new conversation starters. My hope is this unique format helps you to connect more deeply, more often, and more joyfully than ever before.

Barriers to Joy

Another way this journal will help you grow is by assisting you in overcoming a common barrier to joy. In my recent survey, I also asked couples about their greatest challenges. The answer that arose most often was *busyness*. Couples reported having a lack of time, working opposite schedules, struggling with competing priorities, getting sidetracked by the needs of the kids, being distracted by electronic devices, and finding themselves caught up in the whirlwind of life.

People are undoubtedly busier than ever before. Like overcaffeinated fleas, we bounce from one activity to the next, hardly pausing long enough to catch our breath. For those who prefer a different metaphor, you might say we are like a bad amateur plate-spinner, doing our best to keep up, while constantly fearing everything will come crashing down. This is obviously not how love is supposed to work, but it is how countless couples feel.

In many ways, our current busyness epidemic came as a surprise. In 1928, the British economist John Maynard Keynes predicted that scientific advancements and compound interest would render work obsolete. Keynes imagined a society where leisure time was despised, and where labor was longed for. He stated, "It will only be for those who have to do with the singing that life will be tolerable and how few of us can sing! "[2]

Keynes died in 1946, and it is unlikely his prediction will ever come to pass. Although technology has advanced and interest continues to compound, people are now busier than ever. Instead of creating less work, technology and money have generated new forms of entertainment, finer luxuries, added debt, and a non-stop race to keep up.

All of this hustle and bustle is problematic because busyness is the archenemy of relationships. To the human brain, a kind, caring connection to our loved one is on par with food, water, and oxygen—it is a survival need. Our mind does not view busyness as an acceptable excuse for being disconnected. When we feel separated from our spouse, our brain enters into a panicked state.

Recent discoveries show that physical pain and emotional distress cause the same area of our brain—the anterior cingulate cortex or ACC—to light up.[3] This is why feeling separated from our loved one is such a big deal. This study also brings new meaning to the phrase "love hurts." Although it's not actually love that hurts but the inability to be close to someone we long for that generates this turmoil.

Because of our frantic pace, many couples appear sunny on the outside, while a gloomy cloud swells inside. Nowhere is this incongruence more evident than in social media. I've lost count of the number of friends who happily post pictures filled with smiles and joy, only to divorce a short time later. Far too many couples put on a happy front while white-knuckling it on the inside. This incongruence is more prevalent than you might think. Marital happiness is difficult to measure, but experts predict that only 40 percent of couples on the high end, and 17 percent of couples on the low end, are truly happy. And this unhappiness trend is growing increasingly worse.[4]

Because the odds are not in our favor, a routine of connection and intimacy is a must. This journal will help you to break out of the business cycle by building a tiny connection habit into your daily routine. Love is an ongoing process that is strengthened by small moments that compound over time.

Whether you and your loved one are feeling the pain of disconnect or are simply looking for a way to nurture your bond, there is something in this journal for you. By spending a few moments intentionally connecting each day, for an entire year, just imagine how much your relationship will grow. Now it's time to grab a cup of coffee, tea, or another favorite beverage and dive into this creative marriage adventure. I wish you many joyful connection moments in the days ahead!

Sincerely,

[signature]

COFFEE SHOP CONVERSATIONS

January 1

*Looking over the past year, what is one
of your favorite memories, and what made
this experience so meaningful to you?*

Year ____

_____
_____
_____
_____
_____
_____

Year ____

_____
_____
_____
_____
_____
_____

Year ____

_____
_____
_____
_____
_____
_____

January 2

The new year represents a fresh start.
What negative experiences, habits, or relationships
are you looking forward to leaving behind?

Year ___

_____

_____

_____

_____

_____

_____

Year ___

_____

_____

_____

_____

_____

_____

Year ___

_____

_____

_____

_____

_____

_____

January 3

If you summed up last year in either a
single word or a simple phrase, what would it be?
Explain your answer.

Year ___

_____
_____
_____
_____
_____
_____

Year ___

_____
_____
_____
_____
_____
_____

Year ___

_____
_____
_____
_____
_____
_____

January 4

Choose a word to encapsulate your
aspirations for the new year.
Then explain why you chose this word.

Year ___

_____
_____
_____
_____
_____
_____

Year ___

_____
_____
_____
_____
_____
_____

Year ___

_____
_____
_____
_____
_____
_____

January 5

*What new resolution will you
make this year, and why is this
goal important to you?*

Year ____

_____

_____

_____

_____

_____

_____

Year ____

_____

_____

_____

_____

_____

_____

Year ____

_____

_____

_____

_____

_____

_____

January 6

*How can your friends and family
support you in achieving your
New Year's resolution?*

Year ___

_____
_____
_____
_____
_____
_____

Year ___

_____
_____
_____
_____
_____
_____

Year ___

_____
_____
_____
_____
_____
_____

January 7

*Helen Rowland said, "You will never win
if you never begin." What new hobby, skill,
or project will you begin this year?*

Year ____

_____
_____
_____
_____
_____
_____

Year ____

_____
_____
_____
_____
_____
_____

Year ____

_____
_____
_____
_____
_____
_____

January 8

Author Stephen King says, "Books are a uniquely portable magic." What is the best book you read in the last year, and what did you like about it?

Year ___

_____

_____

_____

_____

_____

_____

_____

Year ___

_____

_____

_____

_____

_____

_____

Year ___

_____

_____

_____

_____

_____

_____

January 9

*What goal do you have for
your physical health this year?
Explain why this goal matters to you.*

Year ____

_____
_____
_____
_____
_____
_____

Year ____

_____
_____
_____
_____
_____
_____

Year ____

_____
_____
_____
_____
_____
_____

January 10

*Imagine that each year of your life is written as a chapter
in a book. What would the title of last year's chapter be?
What would be a good title for this year's section?*

Year ___

_____
_____
_____
_____
_____
_____

Year ___

_____
_____
_____
_____
_____
_____

Year ___

_____
_____
_____
_____
_____
_____

January 11

For many people, the new year represents a fresh start.
What negative experiences, habits, or relationships
are you looking forward to leaving behind this year?

Year ____

_____
_____
_____
_____
_____
_____

Year ____

_____
_____
_____
_____
_____
_____

Year ____

_____
_____
_____
_____
_____
_____

January 12

Martin Luther King Jr. said, "Life's most persistent
and urgent question is: What are you doing for others?"
How will you serve others this year?

Year ___

_____
_____
_____
_____
_____
_____

Year ___

_____
_____
_____
_____
_____
_____

Year ___

_____
_____
_____
_____
_____
_____

January 13

What was one of the wisest
choices you made over the last year,
and what impact did this have on your life?

Year ____

_____
_____
_____
_____
_____
_____

Year ____

_____
_____
_____
_____
_____
_____

Year ____

_____
_____
_____
_____
_____
_____

January 14

How can your loved ones
best pray for you
in this new year?

Year ___

_____

_____

_____

_____

_____

_____

Year ___

_____

_____

_____

_____

_____

_____

Year ___

_____

_____

_____

_____

_____

_____

January 15

As you reflect on the past year, what was your biggest time waster? Will you do anything differently this year to make better use of your time?

Year ____

_____
_____
_____
_____
_____
_____

Year ____

_____
_____
_____
_____
_____
_____

Year ____

_____
_____
_____
_____
_____
_____

January 16

If you could have dinner with a
present-day hero, who would it be,
and why?

Year____

_____
_____
_____
_____
_____
_____

Year____

_____
_____
_____
_____
_____
_____

Year____

_____
_____
_____
_____
_____
_____

January 17

Describe a time when you felt especially close to
God this year. Why do you think you felt so close to
Him during this season of life?

Year____

_____

_____

_____

_____

_____

Year____

_____

_____

_____

_____

_____

Year____

_____

_____

_____

_____

_____

January 18

*What are you currently doing to nurture
yourself spiritually? Are there spiritual activities
you did in the past that you miss?*

*Year*____

_____
_____
_____
_____
_____
_____

*Year*____

_____
_____
_____
_____
_____
_____

*Year*____

_____
_____
_____
_____
_____
_____

January 19

*If you could travel
anywhere in the world,
where would go, and why?*

Year ____

_____
_____
_____
_____
_____
_____

Year ____

_____
_____
_____
_____
_____
_____

Year ____

_____
_____
_____
_____
_____
_____

January 20

Describe a major accomplishment
in the past year that you are
especially proud of.

Year ____

_____
_____
_____
_____
_____
_____
_____

Year ____

_____
_____
_____
_____
_____
_____
_____

Year ____

_____
_____
_____
_____
_____
_____
_____

January 21

Who is one couple you admire,
and what qualities make this couple's
relationship great?

Year ____

_____
_____
_____
_____
_____
_____

Year ____

_____
_____
_____
_____
_____
_____

Year ____

_____
_____
_____
_____
_____
_____

January 22

Describe a perfect date night.
Where would you go,
and what would you do?

Year ___

_____

_____

_____

_____

_____

_____

Year ___

_____

_____

_____

_____

_____

_____

Year ___

_____

_____

_____

_____

_____

_____

January 23

When you are in a bad mood,
what is one simple thing your partner
can do to brighten your day?

Year____

_____

_____

_____

_____

_____

Year____

_____

_____

_____

_____

_____

Year____

_____

_____

_____

_____

_____

January 24

*Who is your best friend, and
what do you like most about
your friendship?*

Year ____

_____

_____

_____

_____

_____

_____

Year ____

_____

_____

_____

_____

_____

_____

Year ____

_____

_____

_____

_____

_____

_____

January 25

*If you could have one superpower,
what would it be? How would you use it
to make the world a better place?*

*Year*____

_____
_____
_____
_____
_____
_____

*Year*____

_____
_____
_____
_____
_____
_____

*Year*____

_____
_____
_____
_____
_____
_____

January 26

What are some of life's
simple pleasures that
make you smile?

*Year*____

_____

_____

_____

_____

_____

_____

*Year*____

_____

_____

_____

_____

_____

_____

*Year*____

_____

_____

_____

_____

_____

_____

January 27

*Imagine that you become the president of the United States
for one hour and have the power to enact one law.
What law would you make or change? Why?*

Year____

_____

_____

_____

_____

_____

_____

Year____

_____

_____

_____

_____

_____

_____

Year____

_____

_____

_____

_____

_____

_____

January 28

What is one decision you regret making
this year, and what do you wish
you had done differently?

Year ____

_____

_____

_____

_____

_____

_____

Year ____

_____

_____

_____

_____

_____

_____

Year ____

_____

_____

_____

_____

_____

January 29

*If you created a bucket list, what would your top
three to five items be? If you are answering this question for
the second or third year, be sure to add new items to your bucket list!*

Year____

_____

_____

_____

_____

_____

Year____

_____

_____

_____

_____

_____

Year____

_____

_____

_____

_____

_____

January 30

If you won a thousand dollars today,
would you be more likely to take a vacation,
make a purchase, pay down bills, or save? Why?

Year____

_____
_____
_____
_____
_____
_____

Year____

_____
_____
_____
_____
_____
_____

Year____

_____
_____
_____
_____
_____
_____

January 31

*Who is the happiest
person you know? What do you think
makes this person so upbeat?*

Year ____

_____
_____
_____
_____
_____

Year ____

_____
_____
_____
_____
_____

Year ____

_____
_____
_____
_____
_____

February 1

*Victor Hugo said, "The great acts of love are done by those who
are habitually performing small acts of kindness."
Describe a small act of kindness that made you feel especially loved.*

Year ___

_____
_____
_____
_____
_____
_____

Year ___

_____
_____
_____
_____
_____
_____

Year ___

_____
_____
_____
_____
_____
_____

February 2

*Reflecting on this past week, what are some
small steps you took to show the significant
people in your life that you love them?*

Year ____

_____
_____
_____
_____
_____
_____

Year ____

_____
_____
_____
_____
_____
_____

Year ____

_____
_____
_____
_____
_____
_____

February 3

The word love is a verb or an action word.
First, name some people in your life who love you.
Then share how these people demonstrate their love to you.

Year ____

_____
_____
_____
_____
_____
_____
_____

Year ____

_____
_____
_____
_____
_____
_____
_____

Year ____

_____
_____
_____
_____
_____
_____

February 4

In Matthew 5:44, Jesus said, "Love your enemies."
Share about a recent time you put this Scripture into practice
and were kind to someone mean to you.

Year ____

_____
_____
_____
_____
_____
_____

Year ____

_____
_____
_____
_____
_____
_____

Year ____

_____
_____
_____
_____
_____
_____

February 5

*What is the most romantic movie you saw
in the past year? Describe something
you liked about this movie?*

Year ____

_____
_____
_____
_____
_____
_____

Year ____

_____
_____
_____
_____
_____
_____

Year ____

_____
_____
_____
_____
_____
_____

February 6

How might you show love toward a current rival?
First, share who you are at odds with. Then describe
how you might demonstrate love toward this person.

Year ___

_____
_____
_____
_____
_____
_____

Year ___

_____
_____
_____
_____
_____
_____

Year ___

_____
_____
_____
_____
_____
_____

February 7

*In your opinion, what are some foundational
principles for making a relationship last?
Try to list at least three.*

Year ___

_____
_____
_____
_____
_____
_____

Year ___

_____
_____
_____
_____
_____
_____

Year ___

_____
_____
_____
_____
_____
_____

February 8

Describe your perfect
Valentine's Day.
Be as detailed as possible.

Year ____

_____
_____
_____
_____
_____
_____

Year ____

_____
_____
_____
_____
_____
_____

Year ____

_____
_____
_____
_____
_____
_____

February 9

Would you consider yourself a happy person this year?
If so, how do you stay in a good mood?
If not, what would it take to make you happy?

Year ____

_____

_____

_____

_____

_____

_____

Year ____

_____

_____

_____

_____

_____

_____

Year ____

_____

_____

_____

_____

_____

_____

February 10

*What is the most daring
or dangerous thing
you have done lately?*

Year ____

_____
_____
_____
_____
_____
_____

Year ____

_____
_____
_____
_____
_____
_____

Year ____

_____
_____
_____
_____
_____
_____

February 11

When was the last time you felt loved?
Describe what happened that made
you feel this way.

Year____

_____
_____
_____
_____
_____
_____

Year____

_____
_____
_____
_____
_____
_____

Year____

_____
_____
_____
_____
_____
_____

February 12

Mahatma Gandhi said, "Where there is love there is life." How have you shown love to others this week?

Year _____

_____
_____
_____
_____
_____
_____

Year _____

_____
_____
_____
_____
_____
_____

Year _____

_____
_____
_____
_____
_____
_____

February 13

*What are some of the things you love
about your significant other?
List at least three things.*

Year ___

_____

_____

_____

_____

_____

_____

Year ___

_____

_____

_____

_____

_____

_____

Year ___

_____

_____

_____

_____

_____

_____

February 14

What is something your
loved one introduced you to that
has made your life better?

Year ____

_____
_____
_____
_____
_____
_____

Year ____

_____
_____
_____
_____
_____
_____

Year ____

_____
_____
_____
_____
_____
_____

February 15

Imagine you can ask God any one question.
What would it be, and why? Be sure to come
up with a new question each year.

Year ____

_____
_____
_____
_____
_____
_____

Year ____

_____
_____
_____
_____
_____
_____

Year ____

_____
_____
_____
_____
_____
_____

February 16

*If you gave advice to a
couple who are persistently arguing,
what might you say to them?*

*Year*____

_____

_____

_____

_____

_____

_____

*Year*____

_____

_____

_____

_____

_____

_____

*Year*____

_____

_____

_____

_____

_____

_____

February 17

How do you know if someone is
trustworthy? Do you consider yourself
a trustworthy person?

Year ___

_____
_____
_____
_____
_____
_____

Year ___

_____
_____
_____
_____
_____
_____

Year ___

_____
_____
_____
_____
_____
_____

February 18

*If you were going through a difficult time
and needed to seek out wise advice,
whom would you turn to, and why?*

Year____

_____
_____
_____
_____
_____
_____

Year____

_____
_____
_____
_____
_____

Year____

_____
_____
_____
_____
_____
_____

February 19

What are you currently doing to make this world
a better place? If you cannot think of anything,
what types of things would you like to do in the future?

Year ___

_____

_____

_____

_____

_____

_____

Year ___

_____

_____

_____

_____

_____

_____

Year ___

_____

_____

_____

_____

_____

_____

February 20

Imagine you are listening to your own eulogy.
What types of statements do you hope
are being made about you?

Year ____

_____
_____
_____
_____
_____
_____

Year ____

_____
_____
_____
_____
_____
_____

Year ____

_____
_____
_____
_____
_____
_____

February 21

Who is one person you would like to model your life after?
What specific qualities does this person have that you
want to build into your own life?

Year ___

_____
_____
_____
_____
_____
_____
_____

Year ___

_____
_____
_____
_____
_____
_____
_____

Year ___

_____
_____
_____
_____
_____
_____

February 22

*What do you consider
to be your greatest
strengths?*

Year ____

_____

_____

_____

_____

_____

_____

_____

Year ____

_____

_____

_____

_____

_____

_____

_____

Year ____

_____

_____

_____

_____

_____

_____

February 23

What are some of your
loved one's greatest strengths?
List at least five.

Year ___

_____

_____

_____

_____

_____

_____

Year ___

_____

_____

_____

_____

_____

_____

Year ___

_____

_____

_____

_____

_____

_____

February 24

*Everyone has at least a few
"hot buttons," or little things that
easily annoy them. What are a few of yours?*

Year ___

_____
_____
_____
_____
_____
_____

Year ___

_____
_____
_____
_____
_____
_____

Year ___

_____
_____
_____
_____
_____
_____

February 25

Every family has its own unique culture.
Describe some aspects of your family's culture
that are especially important to you.

Year ___

_____
_____
_____
_____
_____
_____

Year ___

_____
_____
_____
_____
_____
_____

Year ___

_____
_____
_____
_____
_____
_____

February 26

In your opinion, what types of activities does a spiritually healthy couple do together? Are there any spiritual activities that you would like to start doing as a couple?

Year____

_____
_____
_____
_____
_____
_____

Year____

_____
_____
_____
_____
_____
_____

Year____

_____
_____
_____
_____
_____
_____

February 27

Romans 13:10 says, "Love does no wrong
to a neighbor." Who do you need to apologize to,
and how will you do this?

Year ____

_____
_____
_____
_____
_____
_____

Year ____

_____
_____
_____
_____
_____
_____

Year ____

_____
_____
_____
_____
_____
_____

February 28

Have you been a victim of discrimination,
bullying, or racism this year? If so,
what happened, and how did it make you feel?

Year ____

_____
_____
_____
_____
_____
_____

Year ____

_____
_____
_____
_____
_____
_____

Year ____

_____
_____
_____
_____
_____
_____

February 29

*If you had to choose a career
other than the one you are currently in,
what job would you pick, and why?*

*Year*_____

_____
_____
_____
_____
_____
_____

*Year*_____

_____
_____
_____
_____
_____
_____

*Year*_____

_____
_____
_____
_____
_____
_____

March 1

If you and your partner were getting over a big fight,
what is one small step that your spouse could take
to start making amends?

Year____

_____
_____
_____
_____
_____
_____

Year____

_____
_____
_____
_____
_____
_____

Year____

_____
_____
_____
_____
_____
_____

March 2

*If your loved one wanted to do
something simple to show you he
or she cared, what would this look like?*

Year ____

_____
_____
_____
_____
_____
_____

Year ____

_____
_____
_____
_____
_____
_____

Year ____

_____
_____
_____
_____
_____
_____

March 3

*On a scale of one to ten, with one being
not very important and ten being extremely important,
how essential is your faith to you, and why?*

Year ____

_____
_____
_____
_____
_____
_____

Year ____

_____
_____
_____
_____
_____
_____

Year ____

_____
_____
_____
_____
_____
_____

March 4

*If you were to pick a fictional television family
you would most like your own family to resemble,
which family would it be, and why?*

Year ___

_____
_____
_____
_____
_____
_____

Year ___

_____
_____
_____
_____
_____
_____

Year ___

_____
_____
_____
_____
_____
_____

March 5

In your opinion,
what does it mean
for a couple to fight fair?

Year ____

_____

_____

_____

_____

_____

_____

Year ____

_____

_____

_____

_____

_____

_____

Year ____

_____

_____

_____

_____

_____

_____

March 6

In your opinion,
what does it look like when
a couple fights dirty?

Year ____

_____
_____
_____
_____
_____
_____

Year ____

_____
_____
_____
_____
_____
_____

Year ____

_____
_____
_____
_____
_____
_____

March 7

*How would you describe
your conflict style?
Is it fair, dirty, or a mixture of both?*

Year____

_____
_____
_____
_____
_____
_____

Year____

_____
_____
_____
_____
_____
_____

Year____

_____
_____
_____
_____
_____
_____

March 8

What is one conflict you've had that you feel was resolved well? What is it that made your conflict resolution work?

Year ___

_____

_____

_____

_____

_____

_____

Year ___

_____

_____

_____

_____

_____

_____

Year ___

_____

_____

_____

_____

_____

_____

March 9

If you knew you were going to die at this
exact time tomorrow, how would you
spend your last twenty-four hours?

Year ____

_____

_____

_____

_____

_____

_____

Year ____

_____

_____

_____

_____

_____

_____

Year ____

_____

_____

_____

_____

_____

_____

March 10

*Do you believe in
love at first sight?
Why, or why not?*

Year ____

_____

_____

_____

_____

_____

_____

Year ____

_____

_____

_____

_____

_____

_____

Year ____

_____

_____

_____

_____

_____

_____

March 11

*What is one area of our relationship
we could work on together
to make our connection even stronger?*

Year _____

_____

_____

_____

_____

_____

_____

Year _____

_____

_____

_____

_____

_____

_____

Year _____

_____

_____

_____

_____

_____

_____

March 12

What do you think are the
most important things parents can do
to raise great kids?

Year ___

_____
_____
_____
_____
_____
_____

Year ___

_____
_____
_____
_____
_____
_____

Year ___

_____
_____
_____
_____
_____
_____

March 13

*If you could change one thing
about your physical appearance,
what would it be, and why?*

Year ____

_____

_____

_____

_____

_____

_____

Year ____

_____

_____

_____

_____

_____

_____

Year ____

_____

_____

_____

_____

_____

March 14

What do you like best
about our relationship?
List at least three things.

*Year*___

_____

_____

_____

_____

_____

_____

*Year*___

_____

_____

_____

_____

_____

_____

*Year*___

_____

_____

_____

_____

_____

_____

March 15

If you learned that one week from today
you would suddenly lose your ability to see,
how would you spend the next week?

*Year*____

_____
_____
_____
_____
_____
_____

*Year*____

_____
_____
_____
_____
_____
_____

*Year*____

_____
_____
_____
_____
_____

March 16

If you had to choose between a career you love that only pays minimum wage or a job you despise that makes you wealthy, which one would you pick, and why?

Year ____

_____
_____
_____
_____
_____
_____

Year ____

_____
_____
_____
_____
_____
_____

Year ____

_____
_____
_____
_____
_____
_____

March 17

Describe one life experience
that was so amazing you would
relive it again if you could?

Year ___

_____
_____
_____
_____
_____
_____

Year ___

_____
_____
_____
_____
_____
_____

Year ___

_____
_____
_____
_____
_____
_____

March 18

*Describe a challenging experience in your life
that caused you to become a better person?
How did this incident help you improve yourself?*

Year____

_____
_____
_____
_____
_____
_____

Year____

_____
_____
_____
_____
_____
_____

Year____

_____
_____
_____
_____
_____
_____

March 19

Would you describe your life as easy,
average, or
exceptionally difficult? Why?

Year ____

_____
_____
_____
_____
_____
_____

Year ____

_____
_____
_____
_____
_____
_____

Year ____

_____
_____
_____
_____
_____
_____

March 20

What activities bring you
the most joy in life?
List three or more.

Year ____

_____
_____
_____
_____
_____
_____

Year ____

_____
_____
_____
_____
_____
_____

Year ____

_____
_____
_____
_____
_____
_____

March 21

*What life circumstances
cause you
the most pain?*

Year ____

_____
_____
_____
_____
_____
_____

Year ____

_____
_____
_____
_____
_____
_____

Year ____

_____
_____
_____
_____
_____
_____

March 22

*Imagine that you can grant your loved one
any superpower. What amazing ability
would you bestow upon him or her, and why?*

*Year*____

_____
_____
_____
_____
_____
_____

*Year*____

_____
_____
_____
_____
_____
_____

*Year*____

_____
_____
_____
_____
_____
_____

March 23

If you had to relocate to
a different state,
where would you move, and why?

Year ____

_____

_____

_____

_____

_____

_____

Year ____

_____

_____

_____

_____

_____

_____

Year ____

_____

_____

_____

_____

_____

_____

March 24

Imagine you suddenly have the power to turn invisible.
You can go anywhere and do anything, completely unseen.
How will you use this superpower?

Year____

_____
_____
_____
_____
_____
_____

Year____

_____
_____
_____
_____
_____
_____

Year____

_____
_____
_____
_____
_____
_____

March 25

Complete this sentence,
"The three apps on my phone that
I can't live without are..."

Year ____

_____
_____
_____
_____
_____
_____

Year ____

_____
_____
_____
_____
_____
_____

Year ____

_____
_____
_____
_____
_____
_____

March 26

What current activities,
events, or people help you
to feel closer to God?

*Year*____

_____
_____
_____
_____
_____
_____

*Year*____

_____
_____
_____
_____
_____
_____

*Year*____

_____
_____
_____
_____
_____
_____

March 27

Imagine that, like in the movie Groundhog Day,
you will relive the same day over and over again.
What day was so amazing that you would gladly repeat it?

Year ____

_____

_____

_____

_____

_____

_____

Year ____

_____

_____

_____

_____

_____

_____

Year ____

_____

_____

_____

_____

_____

March 28

Randy Pausch says, "The brick walls are not there to keep us out. The brick walls are there to give us a chance to show how badly we want something." What brick wall are you currently facing?

Year ___

_____
_____
_____
_____
_____
_____

Year ___

_____
_____
_____
_____
_____
_____

Year ___

_____
_____
_____
_____
_____
_____

March 29

*What are some ways that your partner
can support you in overcoming your
current brick-wall challenges?*

Year ____

_____
_____
_____
_____
_____
_____

Year ____

_____
_____
_____
_____
_____
_____

Year ____

_____
_____
_____
_____
_____
_____

March 30

*When facing brick walls in your life, are you easily discouraged,
someone who persistently presses forward in spite of challenges,
or are you somewhere in between? Then, explain your answer.*

Year ____

_____
_____
_____
_____
_____
_____

Year ____

_____
_____
_____
_____
_____
_____

Year ____

_____
_____
_____
_____
_____
_____

March 31

*In your family, who excels at optimistically pressing forward
during challenging circumstances? What do you think
is the secret behind this person's persistence?*

Year____

_____
_____
_____
_____
_____
_____

Year____

_____
_____
_____
_____
_____
_____

Year____

_____
_____
_____
_____
_____
_____

April 1

*What is the best April Fool's
joke or practical joke
you had played on you?*

Year ___

_____
_____
_____
_____
_____
_____

Year ___

_____
_____
_____
_____
_____
_____

Year ___

_____
_____
_____
_____
_____
_____

April 2

Describe the best prank
you ever played
on someone else.

Year____

_____

_____

_____

_____

_____

_____

Year____

_____

_____

_____

_____

_____

_____

Year____

_____

_____

_____

_____

_____

_____

April 3

*If your partner wanted to make you feel
especially loved today, what types of things
should he or she do?*

Year ___

_____
_____
_____
_____
_____
_____

Year ___

_____
_____
_____
_____
_____
_____

Year ___

_____
_____
_____
_____
_____
_____

April 4

Describe a happy Easter memory
from childhood. Then share what
made this time so special to you.

Year ____

_____
_____
_____
_____
_____
_____

Year ____

_____
_____
_____
_____
_____
_____

Year ____

_____
_____
_____
_____
_____
_____

April 5

Imagine you find a check for $10,000
in your Easter basket.
How would you spend this money?

Year ____

_____
_____
_____
_____
_____
_____

Year ____

_____
_____
_____
_____
_____
_____

Year ____

_____
_____
_____
_____
_____
_____

April 6

Imagine you can place a $10,000 check in someone else's Easter basket.
The only catch is this person cannot be a family member.
Who would you give this basket to, and why?

Year ____

_____
_____
_____
_____
_____
_____

Year ____

_____
_____
_____
_____
_____
_____

Year ____

_____
_____
_____
_____
_____
_____

April 7

What are some of your favorite
things about spring,
and why do you like them?

*Year*____

_____

_____

_____

_____

_____

_____

*Year*____

_____

_____

_____

_____

_____

_____

*Year*____

_____

_____

_____

_____

_____

_____

April 8

*Who do you know that needs to hear of the hope
that comes through Jesus's death, burial, and resurrection?
How might you share the gospel message with this person?*

Year ____

_____

_____

_____

_____

_____

_____

Year ____

_____

_____

_____

_____

_____

_____

Year ____

_____

_____

_____

_____

_____

_____

April 9

Are you happy with the way you
and your family celebrate Easter now?
If not, what would you like to do differently?

Year ___

_____
_____
_____
_____
_____
_____

Year ___

_____
_____
_____
_____
_____
_____

Year ___

_____
_____
_____
_____
_____
_____

April 10

Reflecting on the past year,
what is the best thing that
happened to you since last Easter?

Year ____

_____
_____
_____
_____
_____
_____

Year ____

_____
_____
_____
_____
_____
_____

Year ____

_____
_____
_____
_____
_____
_____

April 11

*What are some ways you
and your partner honor Christ
in your relationship?*

Year____

_____
_____
_____
_____
_____
_____

Year____

_____
_____
_____
_____
_____
_____

Year____

_____
_____
_____
_____
_____

April 12

*What could you and I start doing to make
our relationship more Christ-honoring? How would
you feel about adding this practice into our bond?*

Year ____

_____
_____
_____
_____
_____
_____

Year ____

_____
_____
_____
_____
_____
_____

Year ____

_____
_____
_____
_____
_____

April 13

When you and your partner are
having fun as a couple,
what activities bring you the most joy?

Year ____

_____

_____

_____

_____

_____

_____

Year ____

_____

_____

_____

_____

_____

_____

Year ____

_____

_____

_____

_____

_____

_____

April 14

What are some activities that bring you less joy,
but you continue to engage in because
you know that it means a lot to your spouse?

Year ____

_____
_____
_____
_____
_____
_____

Year ____

_____
_____
_____
_____
_____
_____

Year ____

_____
_____
_____
_____
_____
_____

April 15

Surprise! You are about to contract a mental illness.
On the bright side, you get to choose which illness this will be.
Which do you pick, and why?

Year____

_____
_____
_____
_____
_____
_____

Year____

_____
_____
_____
_____
_____
_____

Year____

_____
_____
_____
_____
_____
_____

April 16

Who do you know that is stuck in past pain?
What do you think caused him or her to get stuck?
How do you encourage this person?

Year ____

_____
_____
_____
_____
_____
_____

Year ____

_____
_____
_____
_____
_____
_____

Year ____

_____
_____
_____
_____
_____
_____

April 17

Who do you know that has overcome a
painful past? What qualities helped this person
to push past adversity?

*Year*____

_____
_____
_____
_____
_____
_____

*Year*____

_____
_____
_____
_____
_____
_____

*Year*____

_____
_____
_____
_____
_____

April 18

*If your partner noticed you were having
an especially tough day, how would you
want him or her to respond?*

Year ___

_____
_____
_____
_____
_____
_____

Year ___

_____
_____
_____
_____
_____
_____

Year ___

_____
_____
_____
_____
_____

April 19

Children have excellent imaginations.
Describe a childhood game or activity that
delighted you and your friends.

Year ____

_____

_____

_____

_____

_____

_____

_____

Year ____

_____

_____

_____

_____

_____

_____

_____

Year ____

_____

_____

_____

_____

_____

_____

_____

April 20

Imagine the pastor of your church asks you to preach
a sermon on any topic you are passionate about.
What would the theme of your talk be?

Year ____

_____
_____
_____
_____
_____
_____
_____

Year ____

_____
_____
_____
_____
_____
_____
_____

Year ____

_____
_____
_____
_____
_____
_____

April 21

What is one piece of wisdom given to you by a parent,
teacher, coach, or mentor, that stuck with you over time?
Why do you think these words are so meaningful?

Year ____

_____

_____

_____

_____

_____

_____

Year ____

_____

_____

_____

_____

_____

_____

Year ____

_____

_____

_____

_____

_____

_____

April 22

*When is the last time
you laughed aloud,
and what made you laugh?*

Year ____

_____

_____

_____

_____

_____

_____

Year ____

_____

_____

_____

_____

_____

_____

Year ____

_____

_____

_____

_____

_____

_____

April 23

*Imagine you are asked to give advice
to a newly dating couple. What words
of wisdom would you offer, and why?*

Year ____

_____
_____
_____
_____
_____
_____

Year ____

_____
_____
_____
_____
_____
_____

Year ____

_____
_____
_____
_____
_____
_____

April 24

*Describe something
you admire about
your grandparents.*

Year ____

_____
_____
_____
_____
_____
_____

Year ____

_____
_____
_____
_____
_____
_____

Year ____

_____
_____
_____
_____
_____
_____

April 25

*Describe a quality
you admire in
your parents.*

Year ___

_____

_____

_____

_____

_____

_____

Year ___

_____

_____

_____

_____

_____

_____

Year ___

_____

_____

_____

_____

_____

_____

April 26

Describe your happiest moment
over the past week. Why did this
moment bring you so much joy?

Year ____

_____

_____

_____

_____

_____

_____

Year ____

_____

_____

_____

_____

_____

_____

Year ____

_____

_____

_____

_____

_____

_____

April 27

Looking over the past week,
describe your greatest disappointment.
What made this time so discouraging?

Year ____

_____
_____
_____
_____
_____
_____

Year ____

_____
_____
_____
_____
_____
_____

Year ____

_____
_____
_____
_____
_____
_____

April 28

Describe a favorite rainy-day
memory or rainy-day activity
from childhood.

Year ____

_____
_____
_____
_____
_____
_____

Year ____

_____
_____
_____
_____
_____
_____

Year ____

_____
_____
_____
_____
_____
_____

April 29

Imagine you and your loved one are stuck
indoors during a thunderstorm.
Describe what a perfect rainy-day date looks like.

Year____

_____
_____
_____
_____
_____
_____

Year____

_____
_____
_____
_____
_____
_____

Year____

_____
_____
_____
_____
_____
_____

April 30

*Describe a time during the past week when
your partner made you feel important. What did he or she do,
and why did this mean so much to you?*

Year ____

_____
_____
_____
_____
_____
_____

Year ____

_____
_____
_____
_____
_____
_____

Year ____

_____
_____
_____
_____
_____
_____

May 1

What actions have you taken in
the last week to make those
around you feel appreciated?

Year ____

_____

_____

_____

_____

_____

_____

Year ____

_____

_____

_____

_____

_____

_____

Year ____

_____

_____

_____

_____

_____

_____

May 2

*If you could travel back in time
and witness a Biblical miracle,
which one would you most like to see?*

Year ____

_____
_____
_____
_____
_____
_____
_____

Year ____

_____
_____
_____
_____
_____
_____
_____

Year ____

_____
_____
_____
_____
_____
_____
_____

May 3

*If you could return to college
and study any subject,
what would it be, and why?*

*Year*___

_____

_____

_____

_____

_____

_____

*Year*___

_____

_____

_____

_____

_____

_____

*Year*___

_____

_____

_____

_____

_____

_____

May 4

*If your twenty-year-old self traveled
into the future and met you today,
what would he or she think, and why?*

Year ____

_____
_____
_____
_____
_____
_____

Year ____

_____
_____
_____
_____
_____
_____

Year ____

_____
_____
_____
_____
_____
_____

May 5

In 2 Peter 3:16, the Apostle Peter states that some things
in Scripture are difficult to understand.
What Biblical concept confuses or frustrates you?

Year ____

_____
_____
_____
_____
_____
_____

Year ____

_____
_____
_____
_____
_____
_____

Year ____

_____
_____
_____
_____
_____

May 6

What Biblical passage inspires you most?
Why do these verses
mean so much to you personally?

Year ___

_____

_____

_____

_____

_____

_____

Year ___

_____

_____

_____

_____

_____

_____

Year ___

_____

_____

_____

_____

_____

_____

May 7

John Gottman writes about the importance of
repair attempts, or simple actions that reunite a couple
after a quarrel. How do you strive to reconnect with your spouse?

Year ____

_____
_____
_____
_____
_____
_____

Year ____

_____
_____
_____
_____
_____
_____

Year ____

_____
_____
_____
_____
_____
_____

May 8

On a scale of 1-10, how good are you
and your partner at reconnecting after a disagreement?
Explain why you assigned this number.

Year ____

_____

_____

_____

_____

_____

_____

Year ____

_____

_____

_____

_____

_____

_____

Year ____

_____

_____

_____

_____

_____

_____

May 9

*What steps could your loved one
take to make reconnecting after
a disagreement easier?*

Year ____

_____

_____

_____

_____

_____

Year ____

_____

_____

_____

_____

_____

Year ____

_____

_____

_____

_____

_____

May 10

The next time you are upset,
how would you like to manage feelings
of anger, hurt, and sadness?

Year ____

_____
_____
_____
_____
_____
_____

Year ____

_____
_____
_____
_____
_____
_____

Year ____

_____
_____
_____
_____
_____
_____

May 11

As a child, what did you
imagine falling in love
would be like?

Year ___

_____

_____

_____

_____

_____

_____

Year ___

_____

_____

_____

_____

_____

_____

Year ___

_____

_____

_____

_____

_____

_____

May 12

*As an adult,
how do you know
you are in love?*

*Year*____

_____
_____
_____
_____
_____
_____
_____

*Year*____

_____
_____
_____
_____
_____
_____
_____

*Year*____

_____
_____
_____
_____
_____
_____

May 13

What movie did you dislike
so much that you would un-watch
it if you could?

Year ____

_____
_____
_____
_____
_____
_____

Year ____

_____
_____
_____
_____
_____
_____

Year ____

_____
_____
_____
_____
_____
_____

May 14

Imagine a romantic comedy based on your relationship
is being filmed. The director needs a new story
for a funny, idyllic scene. Which story do you tell?

Year ____

_____
_____
_____
_____
_____
_____

Year ____

_____
_____
_____
_____
_____
_____

Year ____

_____
_____
_____
_____
_____
_____

May 15

*What do you consider
to be the most romantic movie
of all time, and why?*

Year ____

_____
_____
_____
_____
_____
_____
_____

Year ____

_____
_____
_____
_____
_____
_____
_____

Year ____

_____
_____
_____
_____
_____
_____

May 16

A popular axiom proclaims,
"A happy wife is a happy life."
Do you agree? Why, or why not?

Year ___

_____
_____
_____
_____
_____
_____

Year ___

_____
_____
_____
_____
_____
_____

Year ___

_____
_____
_____
_____
_____
_____

May 17

What steps do you take
to keep yourself happy
throughout the day?

Year ____

_____

_____

_____

_____

_____

_____

Year ____

_____

_____

_____

_____

_____

_____

Year ____

_____

_____

_____

_____

_____

May 18

*How would you like your partner
to contribute to your happiness? How good
is he or she at doing the things you mentioned?*

Year ____

_____
_____
_____
_____
_____
_____

Year ____

_____
_____
_____
_____
_____
_____

Year ____

_____
_____
_____
_____
_____
_____

May 19

In your opinion, what percentage of your happiness is your responsibility? What percentage is your partner's responsibility? Explain why you assigned these numbers.

Year ____

_____
_____
_____
_____
_____
_____

Year ____

_____
_____
_____
_____
_____
_____

Year ____

_____
_____
_____
_____
_____
_____

May 20

*Complete this sentence,
"In marriage, a husband
should always..."*

Year ____

_____
_____
_____
_____
_____
_____

Year ____

_____
_____
_____
_____
_____
_____

Year ____

_____
_____
_____
_____
_____
_____

May 21

Complete this sentence,
"In marriage, a wife
should always..."

Year ____

_____
_____
_____
_____
_____
_____
_____

Year ____

_____
_____
_____
_____
_____
_____
_____

Year ____

_____
_____
_____
_____
_____
_____

May 22

Finish this sentence,
"In marriage, a husband
should never..."

Year ____

_____
_____
_____
_____
_____
_____

Year ____

_____
_____
_____
_____
_____
_____

Year ____

_____
_____
_____
_____
_____
_____

May 23

Finish this sentence,
"In marriage, a wife
should never..."

Year ____

_____
_____
_____
_____
_____
_____

Year ____

_____
_____
_____
_____
_____
_____

Year ____

_____
_____
_____
_____
_____
_____

May 24

How has your relationship
with your loved one
transformed you for the better?

*Year*____

_____
_____
_____
_____
_____
_____

*Year*____

_____
_____
_____
_____
_____
_____

*Year*____

_____
_____
_____
_____
_____
_____

May 25

Finish this sentence,
"If my 16-year-old self were to see me today,
he or she would feel proud that..."

Year____

_____

_____

_____

_____

_____

_____

Year____

_____

_____

_____

_____

_____

_____

Year____

_____

_____

_____

_____

_____

_____

May 26

*Who is a current mentor
or role model? What do you
admire about this person?*

Year ___

_____
_____
_____
_____
_____
_____

Year ___

_____
_____
_____
_____
_____
_____

Year ___

_____
_____
_____
_____
_____
_____

May 27

Who are you currently mentoring
(or who might you mentor)
and what could this person learn from you?

Year ____

_____
_____
_____
_____
_____
_____

Year ____

_____
_____
_____
_____
_____
_____

Year ____

_____
_____
_____
_____
_____
_____

May 30

Who is acting as Jesus' hands and feet in your life?
First, tell who this person is, then share what he
or she does that is so meaningful to you.

Year ____

_____
_____
_____
_____
_____
_____

Year ____

_____
_____
_____
_____
_____
_____

Year ____

_____
_____
_____
_____
_____
_____

May 31

If you knew you would lose your ability to hear tomorrow,
how would you spend your last day of hearing?
Who would you talk to, what songs would you play, etc.?

Year____

_____
_____
_____
_____
_____
_____

Year____

_____
_____
_____
_____
_____
_____

Year____

_____
_____
_____
_____
_____
_____

June 1

What childhood cartoon
or toy do you hope
comes back in style?

*Year*____

_____

_____

_____

_____

_____

_____

*Year*____

_____

_____

_____

_____

_____

_____

*Year*____

_____

_____

_____

_____

_____

_____

June 2

What is the hardest thing
you did this year, so far?
Would you do it again?

Year____

_____

_____

_____

_____

_____

_____

Year____

_____

_____

_____

_____

_____

_____

Year____

_____

_____

_____

_____

_____

_____

June 3

Which book, outside of the Bible,
has grown your faith the most, and
what was your biggest takeaway?

*Year*___

_____
_____
_____
_____
_____
_____

*Year*___

_____
_____
_____
_____
_____
_____

*Year*___

_____
_____
_____
_____
_____
_____

June 4

If you owned a magical remote that allowed you to
rewind your relationship and change something from the past,
what would you do differently?

Year ____

_____
_____
_____
_____
_____
_____

Year ____

_____
_____
_____
_____
_____
_____

Year ____

_____
_____
_____
_____
_____

June 5

*Describe a time in your relationship where you wished
you had a magical remote control, so you could
push the pause button and make the moment last longer.*

Year____

_____
_____
_____
_____
_____
_____

Year____

_____
_____
_____
_____
_____
_____

Year____

_____
_____
_____
_____
_____
_____

June 6

In the book Strength Finder 2.0, the authors describe how experts excel at their craft by building on their strengths. What are some strengths you see in your spouse?

Year ___

_____

_____

_____

_____

_____

_____

Year ___

_____

_____

_____

_____

_____

_____

Year ___

_____

_____

_____

_____

_____

_____

June 7

*How do your strengths
and your partner's strengths
complement each other?*

Year ____

_____
_____
_____
_____
_____
_____

Year ____

_____
_____
_____
_____
_____
_____

Year ____

_____
_____
_____
_____
_____
_____

June 8

Describe a time that you and your partner
used your strengths to successfully
navigate a dubious situation.

*Year*___

_____

_____

_____

_____

_____

_____

*Year*___

_____

_____

_____

_____

_____

_____

*Year*___

_____

_____

_____

_____

_____

_____

June 9

*Tell a story about something you wanted as a teenager
but were not allowed to have. What was it, why were
you not allowed to have it, and what did you do?*

Year ____

_____
_____
_____
_____
_____
_____

Year ____

_____
_____
_____
_____
_____
_____

Year ____

_____
_____
_____
_____
_____
_____

June 10

If you started an internet blog,
what would you write about,
and what would you name your site?

Year____

Year____

Year____

June 11

What questions have you always wanted
to ask your parents, but never did?
What kept you from asking?

Year____

_____
_____
_____
_____
_____
_____

Year____

_____
_____
_____
_____
_____
_____

Year____

_____
_____
_____
_____
_____
_____

June 12

*Describe a quirky habit
your love one has
that you find endearing.*

*Year*___

_____

_____

_____

_____

_____

_____

*Year*___

_____

_____

_____

_____

_____

_____

*Year*___

_____

_____

_____

_____

_____

_____

June 13

It is said that opposites attract.
What are some opposites
that draw you to your partner?

Year____

_____
_____
_____
_____
_____
_____

Year____

_____
_____
_____
_____
_____
_____

Year____

_____
_____
_____
_____
_____
_____

June 14

Imagine you can eat lunch with anyone currently living,
no matter how famous. Who would you dine with,
and what would you talk about?

Year ____

_____
_____
_____
_____
_____
_____

Year ____

_____
_____
_____
_____
_____
_____

Year ____

_____
_____
_____
_____
_____
_____

June 15

What Biblical character
is most like you?
How are the two of you alike?

Year____

_____
_____
_____
_____
_____
_____

Year____

_____
_____
_____
_____
_____
_____

Year____

_____
_____
_____
_____
_____

June 16

Complete this sentence,
"When you _____, I am blown away
by your love for me."

Year ____

_____
_____
_____
_____
_____
_____

Year ____

_____
_____
_____
_____
_____
_____

Year ____

_____
_____
_____
_____
_____
_____

June 17

Thinking back over your relationship, describe a time
when you felt incredibly loved by your partner.
What made this moment so meaningful to you?

Year ____

_____
_____
_____
_____
_____
_____

Year ____

_____
_____
_____
_____
_____
_____

Year ____

_____
_____
_____
_____
_____
_____

June 18

Describe your motivation for going to work.
Is it purely financial, or are there other things
that attract you to your job?

*Year*___

---

*Year*___

---

*Year*___

June 19

James 1:2 says to count it all joy when you
face trials of all kinds. What trials are you facing,
and how do you find joy amid life's storms?

Year ____

_____
_____
_____
_____
_____
_____

Year ____

_____
_____
_____
_____
_____

Year ____

_____
_____
_____
_____
_____

June 20

Galatians 5:22-23 says, "The fruit of the Spirit is love, joy, peace, patience, kindness, goodness, faithfulness, gentleness, and self-control." How are these fruits present in your life?

Year____

_____

_____

_____

_____

_____

_____

Year____

_____

_____

_____

_____

_____

_____

Year____

_____

_____

_____

_____

_____

_____

June 21

How do you see the fruits of the Spirit,
described in Galatians 5:22-23,
lived out by your spouse?

Year ____

_____
_____
_____
_____
_____
_____

Year ____

_____
_____
_____
_____
_____
_____

Year ____

_____
_____
_____
_____
_____
_____

June 22

Imagine a Hollywood producer wants to make a movie about your relationship. You get to choose the actors. Who should star as you and your spouse, and why?

Year ___

_____
_____
_____
_____
_____
_____

Year ___

_____
_____
_____
_____
_____
_____

Year ___

_____
_____
_____
_____
_____

June 23

If your loved one wanted to surprise
you with your favorite meal,
what should he or she cook?

Year ____

_____
_____
_____
_____
_____
_____

Year ____

_____
_____
_____
_____
_____
_____

Year ____

_____
_____
_____
_____
_____
_____

June 24

What are some of your favoirte
things about summer,
and what do you like about them?

Year ___

_____

_____

_____

_____

_____

_____

Year ___

_____

_____

_____

_____

_____

_____

Year ___

_____

_____

_____

_____

_____

_____

June 25

June 25 marks the half-way point to Christmas.
If Santa offered to give you an early Christmas present,
what would you ask for?

Year ____

_____

_____

_____

_____

_____

_____

Year ____

_____

_____

_____

_____

_____

_____

Year ____

_____

_____

_____

_____

_____

_____

June 26

Quick, name three
qualities that make your
spouse attractive.

Year ____

_____

_____

_____

_____

_____

_____

Year ____

_____

_____

_____

_____

_____

_____

Year ____

_____

_____

_____

_____

_____

_____

June 27

If you could travel back in time
and spend the day with one historical figure,
who would it be, and why?

Year ___

_____
_____
_____
_____
_____
_____

Year ___

_____
_____
_____
_____
_____
_____

Year ___

_____
_____
_____
_____
_____
_____

June 28

*During a presidential election, would you be more likely to
vote for a candidate with the greatest political experience
or the candidate with the strongest moral values? Why?*

Year ___

_____
_____
_____
_____
_____
_____

Year ___

_____
_____
_____
_____
_____
_____

Year ___

_____
_____
_____
_____
_____
_____

June 29

*If you had to choose between going through
the rest of your life not being able to see or not
being able to hear, which would you choose, and why?*

Year ____

_____
_____
_____
_____
_____
_____

Year ____

_____
_____
_____
_____
_____
_____

Year ____

_____
_____
_____
_____
_____
_____

June 30

Describe a simple
pleasure that made
you happy today.

Year ___

_____

_____

_____

_____

_____

_____

Year ___

_____

_____

_____

_____

_____

_____

Year ___

_____

_____

_____

_____

_____

_____

July 1

*What is the kindest thing
that someone did for you
this week?*

Year ____

_____

_____

_____

_____

_____

_____

Year ____

_____

_____

_____

_____

_____

_____

Year ____

_____

_____

_____

_____

_____

_____

July 2

How have you been
kind to someone else
this week?

Year ____

_____
_____
_____
_____
_____
_____

Year ____

_____
_____
_____
_____
_____
_____

Year ____

_____
_____
_____
_____
_____
_____

July 3

*When it comes to finances, are you
more of a saver or a spender,
and has this changed over time?*

*Year*____

_____
_____
_____
_____
_____
_____

*Year*____

_____
_____
_____
_____
_____
_____

*Year*____

_____
_____
_____
_____
_____
_____

July 4

*What are some freedoms
that you are especially
grateful for?*

Year ____

_____
_____
_____
_____
_____
_____

Year ____

_____
_____
_____
_____
_____
_____

Year ____

_____
_____
_____
_____
_____

July 5

If you could choose the next president,
who would you appoint,
and why?

Year ____

_____
_____
_____
_____
_____
_____

Year ____

_____
_____
_____
_____
_____
_____

Year ____

_____
_____
_____
_____
_____
_____

July 6

An old axiom says,
"It is better to give than to receive."
Do you believe this is true? Why, or why not?

Year____

_____

_____

_____

_____

_____

Year____

_____

_____

_____

_____

_____

Year____

_____

_____

_____

_____

_____

July 7

If you created a bucket list today,
what would be your top three things
to see or do before "kicking the bucket?"

Year ____

_____
_____
_____
_____
_____
_____

Year ____

_____
_____
_____
_____
_____
_____

Year ____

_____
_____
_____
_____
_____
_____

July 8

If you could give one piece of advice
to our current president,
what would it be?

Year ____

_____
_____
_____
_____
_____
_____

Year ____

_____
_____
_____
_____
_____
_____

Year ____

_____
_____
_____
_____
_____
_____

July 9

*What do you think happens
to people immediately
after they die?*

*Year*____

_____
_____
_____
_____
_____
_____

*Year*____

_____
_____
_____
_____
_____
_____

*Year*____

_____
_____
_____
_____
_____

July 10

If you had Superman's ability to
fly for a day, where would you go,
and what would you do?

Year ___

_____
_____
_____
_____
_____
_____

Year ___

_____
_____
_____
_____
_____
_____

Year ___

_____
_____
_____
_____
_____
_____

July 11

*When was the last time
you said the words "I'm sorry,"
and what did you apologize for?*

Year____

_____
_____
_____
_____
_____
_____

Year____

_____
_____
_____
_____
_____
_____

Year____

_____
_____
_____
_____
_____
_____

July 12

*What song makes
you want to dance
the most?*

Year____

_____
_____
_____
_____
_____
_____

Year____

_____
_____
_____
_____
_____
_____

Year____

_____
_____
_____
_____
_____
_____

July 13

What family member do you look up to,
and what specifically
do you admire about this person?

Year____

_____
_____
_____
_____
_____
_____

Year____

_____
_____
_____
_____
_____
_____

Year____

_____
_____
_____
_____
_____
_____

July 14

Finish this sentence:
"The best part about
being me is..."

Year____

_____
_____
_____
_____
_____
_____

Year____

_____
_____
_____
_____
_____
_____

Year____

_____
_____
_____
_____
_____
_____

July 15

Complete this sentence:
"Something difficult about
being me is..."

Year ____

_____
_____
_____
_____
_____
_____

Year ____

_____
_____
_____
_____
_____
_____

Year ____

_____
_____
_____
_____
_____
_____

July 16

Who are some of your closest friends,
and why are these friendships
important to you?

Year____

_____
_____
_____
_____
_____
_____

Year____

_____
_____
_____
_____
_____
_____

Year____

_____
_____
_____
_____
_____

July 17

What cartoon character has a
personality most like your own,
and what makes the two of your alike?

Year ____

_____
_____
_____
_____
_____
_____
_____

Year ____

_____
_____
_____
_____
_____
_____
_____

Year ____

_____
_____
_____
_____
_____
_____

July 18

Complete this sentence:
"A food I would be perfectly
happy never eating again is..."

Year ____

_____

_____

_____

_____

_____

Year ____

_____

_____

_____

_____

_____

Year ____

_____

_____

_____

_____

_____

July 19

Theodore Roosevelt said, "The only man who never makes a mistake is the man who never does anything." What mistake are you learning from?

Year____

_____
_____
_____
_____
_____
_____

Year____

_____
_____
_____
_____
_____
_____

Year____

_____
_____
_____
_____
_____
_____

July 20

*Which of The Seven Dwarfs best describes you
today—Bashful, Dopey, Sleepy, Sneezy,
Grumpy, Happy, or Doc, and why?*

Year____

_____
_____
_____
_____
_____
_____

Year____

_____
_____
_____
_____
_____
_____

Year____

_____
_____
_____
_____
_____
_____

July 21

*If you could donate a million dollars
to any charitable organization,
which would you choose and why?*

Year____

_____
_____
_____
_____
_____
_____

Year____

_____
_____
_____
_____
_____
_____

Year____

_____
_____
_____
_____
_____
_____

July 22

Imagine a rich relative gives you a million dollars
to spend any way you like.
What is the first purchase you would make?

Year____

_____

_____

_____

_____

_____

_____

Year____

_____

_____

_____

_____

_____

_____

Year____

_____

_____

_____

_____

_____

_____

July 23

*Quick, name three
things that brought
you joy this week—go!*

Year ____

_____
_____
_____
_____
_____
_____

Year ____

_____
_____
_____
_____
_____
_____

Year ____

_____
_____
_____
_____
_____
_____

July 24

What is one thing that happened this week
that was frustrating or annoying?
Even a small frustration counts.

Year____

_____
_____
_____
_____
_____
_____

Year____

_____
_____
_____
_____
_____
_____

Year____

_____
_____
_____
_____
_____
_____

July 25

Finish this sentence:
"The most stressful part
about being me is..."

Year____

_____
_____
_____
_____
_____
_____

Year____

_____
_____
_____
_____
_____
_____

Year____

_____
_____
_____
_____
_____
_____

July 26

If you could only enjoy
three different snack foods
for the rest of your life, what would they be?

Year ____

_____
_____
_____
_____
_____
_____

Year ____

_____
_____
_____
_____
_____
_____

Year ____

_____
_____
_____
_____
_____
_____

July 27

*When you feel sad, mad,
or frustrated, what activities
make you smile again?*

Year____

_____
_____
_____
_____
_____
_____
_____

Year____

_____
_____
_____
_____
_____
_____

Year____

_____
_____
_____
_____
_____
_____

July 28

Who is the bravest person
you know, and what do you think
makes this person so brave?

Year ____

_____
_____
_____
_____
_____
_____

Year ____

_____
_____
_____
_____
_____
_____

Year ____

_____
_____
_____
_____
_____
_____

July 29

*Walt Disney said, "If you can dream it,
you can do it." If you knew, without a doubt,
that you would not fail, what would you do?*

Year____

_____
_____
_____
_____
_____
_____
_____

Year____

_____
_____
_____
_____
_____
_____
_____

Year____

_____
_____
_____
_____
_____
_____

July 30

*Name one movie you think everyone
ought to see. Then explain why
people need to watch this movie.*

Year ____

_____
_____
_____
_____
_____
_____

Year ____

_____
_____
_____
_____
_____
_____

Year ____

_____
_____
_____
_____
_____
_____

July 31

*Would you ever consider living in a
different country? For what reasons would
you be willing to move?*

Year ____

_____
_____
_____
_____
_____
_____

Year ____

_____
_____
_____
_____
_____
_____

Year ____

_____
_____
_____
_____
_____

August 1

Who is the happiest couple that you know?
In your opinion, what makes this couple's
relationship work so well?

Year ____

_____

_____

_____

_____

_____

_____

Year ____

_____

_____

_____

_____

_____

_____

Year ____

_____

_____

_____

_____

_____

_____

August 2

On a scale of 1-10, with 1 being miserable
and 10 being ecstatic, how happy are you
at your present job? Why?

Year ____

_____

_____

_____

_____

_____

_____

Year ____

_____

_____

_____

_____

_____

_____

Year ____

_____

_____

_____

_____

_____

August 3

*Where do you dream
about working ten years
from now?*

*Year*____

_____

_____

_____

_____

_____

_____

_____

*Year*____

_____

_____

_____

_____

_____

_____

_____

*Year*____

_____

_____

_____

_____

_____

_____

_____

August 4

*What ingredients do you
think are necessary for
a lifetime of love?*

Year ____

_____
_____
_____
_____
_____
_____

Year ____

_____
_____
_____
_____
_____
_____

Year ____

_____
_____
_____
_____
_____
_____

August 5

Michael Leunig said, "Love one another
and you will be happy. It's as simple and as difficult as that."
Do you agree or disagree, and why?

Year ___

_____

_____

_____

_____

_____

_____

Year ___

_____

_____

_____

_____

_____

_____

Year ___

_____

_____

_____

_____

_____

_____

August 6

Describe a vacation
you plan to take within
the next year.

*Year*____

_____
_____
_____
_____
_____
_____

*Year*____

_____
_____
_____
_____
_____
_____

*Year*____

_____
_____
_____
_____
_____
_____

August 7

Describe a dream vacation
you hope to take within
the next ten years.

Year ____

_____

_____

_____

_____

_____

_____

Year ____

_____

_____

_____

_____

_____

_____

Year ____

_____

_____

_____

_____

_____

_____

August 8

*Imagine waking up and discovering
work has given you a paid day off.
How would you spend the day?*

Year____

_____
_____
_____
_____
_____
_____

Year____

_____
_____
_____
_____
_____
_____

Year____

_____
_____
_____
_____
_____
_____

August 9

*What are three qualities
that make your spouse
a good friend?*

Year ___

_____
_____
_____
_____
_____
_____

Year ___

_____
_____
_____
_____
_____
_____

Year ___

_____
_____
_____
_____
_____
_____

August 10

*Imagine a rich relative offers to buy you
a new car—any one you choose!
What would your next vehicle be?*

Year____

_____

_____

_____

_____

_____

_____

Year____

_____

_____

_____

_____

_____

_____

Year____

_____

_____

_____

_____

_____

_____

August 11

*What activities
do you wish we did
more often?*

*Year*____

_____

_____

_____

_____

_____

_____

*Year*____

_____

_____

_____

_____

_____

_____

*Year*____

_____

_____

_____

_____

_____

_____

August 12

*Do you consider yourself
an affectionate person?
Why or why not?*

Year____

_____

_____

_____

_____

_____

_____

Year____

_____

_____

_____

_____

_____

_____

Year____

_____

_____

_____

_____

_____

_____

August 13

Are you more prone
to follow your head or your heart
when making big decisions, and why?

*Year*____

_____

_____

_____

_____

_____

_____

*Year*____

_____

_____

_____

_____

_____

_____

*Year*____

_____

_____

_____

_____

_____

_____

August 14

Approximately half of
first marriages end in divorce.
Why do you think this is the case?

Year____

_____
_____
_____
_____
_____
_____

Year____

_____
_____
_____
_____
_____
_____

Year____

_____
_____
_____
_____
_____

August 15

Why will your marriage defy the dismal
divorce statistics and brilliantly succeed?
List three reasons or more.

Year ____

_____

_____

_____

_____

_____

_____

Year ____

_____

_____

_____

_____

_____

_____

Year ____

_____

_____

_____

_____

_____

_____

August 16

When you and your spouse go through
challenging times, who will you look to
for wisdom and support?

Year ____

_____
_____
_____
_____
_____
_____

Year ____

_____
_____
_____
_____
_____
_____

Year ____

_____
_____
_____
_____
_____
_____

August 17

Imagine you have a horrendous day.
How would you like your spouse
to encourage and support you?

*Year*___

_____
_____
_____
_____
_____
_____

*Year*___

_____
_____
_____
_____
_____
_____

*Year*___

_____
_____
_____
_____
_____
_____

August 18

What is a favorite nonfiction book,
and what is something important
this book taught you?

Year ____

_____

_____

_____

_____

_____

_____

Year ____

_____

_____

_____

_____

_____

_____

Year ____

_____

_____

_____

_____

_____

_____

August 19

Do you believe in the adage,
"A penny saved is a penny earned"?
Why or why not?

Year____

_____

_____

_____

_____

_____

_____

Year____

_____

_____

_____

_____

_____

_____

Year____

_____

_____

_____

_____

_____

_____

August 20

Imagine your birthday is declared
a national holiday. Describe how you would
like people to celebrate you.

Year _____

_____
_____
_____
_____
_____
_____

Year _____

_____
_____
_____
_____
_____
_____

Year _____

_____
_____
_____
_____
_____
_____

August 21

*Judy Garland said, "For it was not into my ear you whispered,
but into my heart." How does your spouse
whisper into your heart?*

Year ____

_____

_____

_____

_____

_____

_____

Year ____

_____

_____

_____

_____

_____

_____

Year ____

_____

_____

_____

_____

_____

_____

August 22

*What are you doing this month
to further your personal
growth and development?*

Year____

_____
_____
_____
_____
_____
_____

Year____

_____
_____
_____
_____
_____
_____

Year____

_____
_____
_____
_____
_____
_____

August 23

What is a favorite fiction book?
What about this story piqued
your interest?

Year ____

_____
_____
_____
_____
_____
_____

Year ____

_____
_____
_____
_____
_____
_____

Year ____

_____
_____
_____
_____
_____
_____

August 24

*How can your spouse encourage
and support you in your
personal growth?*

Year ___

_____

_____

_____

_____

_____

_____

Year ___

_____

_____

_____

_____

_____

_____

Year ___

_____

_____

_____

_____

_____

_____

August 25

When you feel stressed,
what activities help you
to relax?

Year____

_____
_____
_____
_____
_____
_____

Year____

_____
_____
_____
_____
_____
_____

Year____

_____
_____
_____
_____
_____
_____

August 26

Your house is on fire! Fortunately, everyone is safe.
Unfortunately, you only have time to grab three personal items.
What do you take with you?

Year ____

_____

_____

_____

_____

_____

_____

Year ____

_____

_____

_____

_____

_____

_____

Year ____

_____

_____

_____

_____

_____

_____

August 27

*You can choose any musical group to play
at your party. What band do you pick,
and what opening song will they play?*

Year ____

_____
_____
_____
_____
_____
_____

Year ____

_____
_____
_____
_____
_____
_____

Year ____

_____
_____
_____
_____
_____
_____

August 28

Imagine that you must abolish one holiday—meaning
no one will be allowed to celebrate this day again.
Which holiday do you eliminate, and why?

Year____

_____
_____
_____
_____
_____
_____

Year____

_____
_____
_____
_____
_____
_____

Year____

_____
_____
_____
_____
_____
_____

August 29

*What is your favorite
comfort food, and when was
the last time you enjoyed it?*

*Year*___

_____
_____
_____
_____
_____
_____
_____

*Year*___

_____
_____
_____
_____
_____
_____
_____

*Year*___

_____
_____
_____
_____
_____
_____

August 30

Surprise, you get to choose your allergies!
What two foods will you be allergic to
for the rest of your life?

Year ____

_____
_____
_____
_____
_____
_____

Year ____

_____
_____
_____
_____
_____
_____

Year ____

_____
_____
_____
_____
_____
_____

August 31

Complete this sentence:
"One app, video game, or computer program
I cannot live without is..."

Year____

_____

_____

_____

_____

_____

_____

Year____

_____

_____

_____

_____

_____

_____

Year____

_____

_____

_____

_____

_____

_____

September 1

*How adventurous do you feel today? A one means,
"Watching The Discovery Channel is as adventurous as I get."
A ten means, "You name it, and I'll do it!"*

Year ____

_____
_____
_____
_____
_____
_____

Year ____

_____
_____
_____
_____
_____
_____

Year ____

_____
_____
_____
_____
_____
_____

September 2

*If everyone referred to you by
your favorite nickname today,
what would they call you?*

Year ____

_____
_____
_____
_____
_____
_____

Year ____

_____
_____
_____
_____
_____
_____

Year ____

_____
_____
_____
_____
_____
_____

September 3

Finish this sentence:
"An unusual talent
I have is..."

Year____

_____
_____
_____
_____
_____
_____

Year____

_____
_____
_____
_____
_____
_____

Year____

_____
_____
_____
_____
_____
_____

September 4

Tell a story about a time you
were embarrassed. Who was involved,
and what happened?

Year____

_____
_____
_____
_____
_____
_____

Year____

_____
_____
_____
_____
_____
_____

Year____

_____
_____
_____
_____
_____
_____

September 5

If you could travel back in time
and give one piece of advice to your younger self,
what advice would you give?

Year ____

_____
_____
_____
_____
_____
_____

Year ____

_____
_____
_____
_____
_____
_____

Year ____

_____
_____
_____
_____
_____
_____

September 6

Finish this sentence.
"Parents should
always..."

*Year*____

_____

_____

_____

_____

_____

_____

*Year*____

_____

_____

_____

_____

_____

_____

*Year*____

_____

_____

_____

_____

_____

_____

September 7

Finish this sentence.
"Parents should
never..."

Year ____

_____

_____

_____

_____

_____

_____

Year ____

_____

_____

_____

_____

_____

_____

Year ____

_____

_____

_____

_____

_____

_____

September 8

*If you could spend the day
binge-watching any television series,
what show would it be?*

Year ____

_____
_____
_____
_____
_____
_____

Year ____

_____
_____
_____
_____
_____
_____

Year ____

_____
_____
_____
_____
_____
_____

September 9

*What movie do you hope
they make a sequel to,
soon?*

Year____

_____
_____
_____
_____
_____
_____
_____

Year____

_____
_____
_____
_____
_____
_____
_____

Year____

_____
_____
_____
_____
_____
_____
_____

September 10

When you get sick,
how do you like your spouse
to care for you?

*Year*___

_____
_____
_____
_____
_____
_____
_____

*Year*___

_____
_____
_____
_____
_____
_____
_____

*Year*___

_____
_____
_____
_____
_____
_____

September 11

What is one thing you remember doing on 9/11/2001,
and how do you commemorate the victims
of the 9/11 attack?

Year____

_____

_____

_____

_____

_____

_____

Year____

_____

_____

_____

_____

_____

Year____

_____

_____

_____

_____

_____

September 12

If you had the option of going skydiving,
scuba diving, or staying home and watching television.
What activity would you choose, and why?

*Year*____

_____
_____
_____
_____
_____
_____
_____

*Year*____

_____
_____
_____
_____
_____
_____

*Year*____

_____
_____
_____
_____
_____
_____

September 13

Surprise, you get to compete on
any game show you want!
Which will you choose, and why?

Year____

_____
_____
_____
_____
_____
_____

Year____

_____
_____
_____
_____
_____
_____

Year____

_____
_____
_____
_____
_____
_____

September 14

*What bad habit
are you currently
trying to break?*

*Year*____

_____
_____
_____
_____
_____
_____
_____

*Year*____

_____
_____
_____
_____
_____
_____
_____

*Year*____

_____
_____
_____
_____
_____
_____
_____

September 15

*What is one
healthy habit
you have?*

*Year*____

_____
_____
_____
_____
_____
_____

*Year*____

_____
_____
_____
_____
_____
_____

*Year*____

_____
_____
_____
_____
_____
_____

September 16

You are about to be stranded on a tropical island
for a year. The bright side is you can take one
luxury item with you. What will you bring, and why?

Year ___

_____

_____

_____

_____

_____

_____

Year ___

_____

_____

_____

_____

_____

_____

Year ___

_____

_____

_____

_____

_____

_____

September 17

*On a scale of 1-10, how happy
are you with your physical appearance,
and why?*

Year ____

_____

_____

_____

_____

_____

_____

Year ____

_____

_____

_____

_____

_____

_____

Year ____

_____

_____

_____

_____

_____

_____

September 18

Thinking back over the last week,
what are some big and small ways
your spouse demonstrated love for you?

Year ____

_____
_____
_____
_____
_____
_____

Year ____

_____
_____
_____
_____
_____
_____

Year ____

_____
_____
_____
_____
_____

September 19

Describe a favorite
romantic date with your spouse.
What made this time so meaningful?

Year ____

_____

_____

_____

_____

_____

_____

Year ____

_____

_____

_____

_____

_____

_____

Year ____

_____

_____

_____

_____

_____

_____

September 20

You are about to be stranded on a deserted island for a year.
You get to bring one—and only one—book with you.
Which do you choose, and why?

Year ___

_____
_____
_____
_____
_____
_____
_____

Year ___

_____
_____
_____
_____
_____
_____
_____

Year ___

_____
_____
_____
_____
_____
_____
_____

September 21

*What movie is so bad that
it should never, under any circumstances,
have a sequel made?*

Year____

_____
_____
_____
_____
_____
_____

Year____

_____
_____
_____
_____
_____
_____

Year____

_____
_____
_____
_____
_____
_____

September 22

Imagine you find a magic lamp.
The genie offers to grant you three wishes
for your marriage. What do you wish for?

Year ___

_____

_____

_____

_____

_____

_____

Year ___

_____

_____

_____

_____

_____

_____

Year ___

_____

_____

_____

_____

_____

_____

September 23

Describe a time when God answered
your prayer. What did you pray for,
and how did God provide?

Year ____

_____
_____
_____
_____
_____
_____

Year ____

_____
_____
_____
_____
_____
_____

Year ____

_____
_____
_____
_____
_____
_____

September 24

*When was the last time
you prayed, and what
did you pray about?*

Year ____

_____
_____
_____
_____
_____
_____

Year ____

_____
_____
_____
_____
_____
_____

Year ____

_____
_____
_____
_____
_____
_____

September 25

How can your
spouse best pray
for you today?

Year ____

_____

_____

_____

_____

_____

_____

Year ____

_____

_____

_____

_____

_____

_____

Year ____

_____

_____

_____

_____

_____

_____

September 26

Do you ever lay awake at
night worried? If so,
what causes you to stress?

Year____

_____
_____
_____
_____
_____
_____
_____

Year____

_____
_____
_____
_____
_____
_____
_____

Year____

_____
_____
_____
_____
_____
_____

September 27

What quote or piece of advice
do you try to live by?
Why does this statement resonate with you?

Year_____

_____
_____
_____
_____
_____
_____

Year_____

_____
_____
_____
_____
_____
_____

Year_____

_____
_____
_____
_____
_____
_____

September 28

Finish this sentence:
"The world would be
a better place if..."

Year ___

_____

_____

_____

_____

_____

_____

Year ___

_____

_____

_____

_____

_____

_____

Year ___

_____

_____

_____

_____

_____

_____

September 29

*In your opinion, what is
the perfect combination
of pizza toppings?*

Year ___

_____
_____
_____
_____
_____
_____

Year ___

_____
_____
_____
_____
_____
_____

Year ___

_____
_____
_____
_____
_____
_____

September 30

Helen Keller said, "Life is either a daring adventure
or nothing." What makes your life
a daring adventure?

Year ____

_____

_____

_____

_____

_____

_____

Year ____

_____

_____

_____

_____

_____

_____

Year ____

_____

_____

_____

_____

_____

_____

October 1

Who is a favorite fictional hero,
and what do you admire
about this person?

*Year*___

_____
_____
_____
_____
_____
_____

*Year*___

_____
_____
_____
_____
_____
_____

*Year*___

_____
_____
_____
_____
_____
_____

October 2

Bill Gates said, "Most people overestimate what
they can do in one year and underestimate what they can do
in ten years." What big, ten-year goals do you have?

Year _____

_____
_____
_____
_____
_____
_____

Year _____

_____
_____
_____
_____
_____
_____

Year _____

_____
_____
_____
_____
_____
_____

October 3

Eleanor Roosevelt said, "Do one thing
every day that scares you."
What will you do today that scares you?

Year____

_____
_____
_____
_____
_____
_____
_____

Year____

_____
_____
_____
_____
_____
_____
_____

Year____

_____
_____
_____
_____
_____
_____

October 4

Quick, share three
things that you love
about your spouse.

Year ___

_____
_____
_____
_____
_____
_____
_____

Year ___

_____
_____
_____
_____
_____
_____
_____

Year ___

_____
_____
_____
_____
_____
_____
_____

October 5

*Bruce Lee said, "Simplicity is the key
to brilliance." Name three simple
pleasures you plan to enjoy today?*

Year ____

_____

_____

_____

_____

_____

_____

Year ____

_____

_____

_____

_____

_____

_____

Year ____

_____

_____

_____

_____

_____

_____

October 6

*Dr. Seuss said, "Don't cry because it's over,
smile because it happened." When was the last time
you felt happy, and what made you feel this way?*

Year____

_____

_____

_____

_____

_____

_____

Year____

_____

_____

_____

_____

_____

_____

Year____

_____

_____

_____

_____

_____

_____

October 7

Share a favorite memory you had
with your spouse this week?
What made this experience so meaningful?

Year____

_____
_____
_____
_____
_____
_____

Year____

_____
_____
_____
_____
_____
_____

Year____

_____
_____
_____
_____
_____
_____

October 8

*Would you rather be able to fly
or turn invisible? How would you use
this superpower for good?*

Year____

_____
_____
_____
_____
_____
_____

Year____

_____
_____
_____
_____
_____
_____

Year____

_____
_____
_____
_____
_____
_____

October 9

*If you and your spouse
started a business together,
what would it be?*

Year____

_____
_____
_____
_____
_____
_____

Year____

_____
_____
_____
_____
_____
_____

Year____

_____
_____
_____
_____
_____
_____

October 10

Describe
your dream
home.

Year ___

_____

_____

_____

_____

_____

_____

Year ___

_____

_____

_____

_____

_____

_____

Year ___

_____

_____

_____

_____

_____

_____

October 11

*What is the most
spontaneous thing you've
done in the last month.*

Year ____

_____
_____
_____
_____
_____
_____

Year ____

_____
_____
_____
_____
_____
_____

Year ____

_____
_____
_____
_____
_____
_____

October 12

*What are some things
you've learned about
yourself lately?*

Year____

_____
_____
_____
_____
_____
_____

Year____

_____
_____
_____
_____
_____
_____

Year____

_____
_____
_____
_____
_____
_____

October 13

*Howard Thurman said, "Don't ask yourself what
the world needs. Ask yourself what makes you come alive."
What makes you feel alive?*

Year____

_____
_____
_____
_____
_____
_____

Year____

_____
_____
_____
_____
_____
_____

Year____

_____
_____
_____
_____
_____
_____

October 14

*On a scale of 1-10, with one being incredibly relaxed
and ten being overwhelmingly stressed,
what is your overall level of stress this week, and why?*

Year ___

_____
_____
_____
_____
_____
_____

Year ___

_____
_____
_____
_____
_____
_____

Year ___

_____
_____
_____
_____
_____
_____

October 15

*What accomplishment
are you most proud of
this week?*

Year____

_____

_____

_____

_____

_____

_____

_____

Year____

_____

_____

_____

_____

_____

_____

_____

Year____

_____

_____

_____

_____

_____

_____

_____

October 16

*If you could travel back in time and ask
a Biblical figure for marriage advice, who would
you meet with, and what would you ask?*

Year ___

_____
_____
_____
_____
_____
_____
_____

Year ___

_____
_____
_____
_____
_____
_____
_____

Year ___

_____
_____
_____
_____
_____
_____
_____

October 17

What video game does every
adult need to play at least once
in their lifetime?

Year ____

_____
_____
_____
_____
_____
_____

Year ____

_____
_____
_____
_____
_____
_____

Year ____

_____
_____
_____
_____
_____
_____

October 18

*What future activity, vacation,
or event are you most excited
about right now?*

Year ____

_____
_____
_____
_____
_____
_____
_____

Year ____

_____
_____
_____
_____
_____
_____
_____

Year ____

_____
_____
_____
_____
_____
_____

October 19

*What is your least
favorite form of exercise,
and why?*

Year ___

_____

_____

_____

_____

_____

_____

Year ___

_____

_____

_____

_____

_____

_____

Year ___

_____

_____

_____

_____

_____

_____

October 20

Anthony Brandt said, "Other things may change us,
but we start and end with family."
Describe something you love about your family.

Year ____

_____

_____

_____

_____

_____

_____

Year ____

_____

_____

_____

_____

_____

_____

Year ____

_____

_____

_____

_____

_____

_____

October 21

*What flavor of ice cream
would you gladly eat every day
for an entire year?*

Year____

_____
_____
_____
_____
_____
_____
_____

Year____

_____
_____
_____
_____
_____
_____

Year____

_____
_____
_____
_____
_____
_____

October 22

What dessert or meal would
you like to learn
how to cook in the future?

*Year*____

_____

_____

_____

_____

_____

_____

*Year*____

_____

_____

_____

_____

_____

_____

*Year*____

_____

_____

_____

_____

_____

_____

October 23

You are a guest contestant on a reality cooking show
and asked to whip up your specialty.
Describe your specialty.

Year ____

_____

_____

_____

_____

_____

_____

Year ____

_____

_____

_____

_____

_____

_____

Year ____

_____

_____

_____

_____

_____

_____

October 24

What did you do in the last month
to make the world a better place?
Even a little act is OK.

Year____

_____

_____

_____

_____

_____

_____

Year____

_____

_____

_____

_____

_____

_____

Year____

_____

_____

_____

_____

_____

_____

October 25

Which pieces of Halloween candy do you always eat first?
For years two and three, share your
second and third favorite Halloween treat.

*Year*____

_____

_____

_____

_____

_____

_____

*Year*____

_____

_____

_____

_____

_____

_____

*Year*____

_____

_____

_____

_____

_____

_____

October 26

*Do you usually remember your dreams
or forget them? If you remember them,
describe one dream you can easily recall.*

*Year*___

_____
_____
_____
_____
_____
_____

*Year*___

_____
_____
_____
_____
_____
_____

*Year*___

_____
_____
_____
_____
_____
_____

October 27

*It's National Mentoring Day. If you could choose
a famous person to mentor you for a day, who would it be,
and what would you ask this person to teach you?*

Year____

_____
_____
_____
_____
_____
_____

Year____

_____
_____
_____
_____
_____
_____

Year____

_____
_____
_____
_____
_____
_____

October 28

Describe a favorite
Halloween costume from the past.
What did you like about it?

Year____

_____

_____

_____

_____

_____

_____

Year____

_____

_____

_____

_____

_____

_____

Year____

_____

_____

_____

_____

_____

_____

October 29

*Will you dress up
for Halloween this year?
Why, or why not?*

*Year*____

_____
_____
_____
_____
_____
_____

*Year*____

_____
_____
_____
_____
_____
_____

*Year*____

_____
_____
_____
_____
_____
_____

October 30

*What irrational fears
or phobias do you
possess?*

*Year*____

_____

_____

_____

_____

_____

_____

_____

*Year*____

_____

_____

_____

_____

_____

_____

_____

*Year*____

_____

_____

_____

_____

_____

_____

_____

October 31

*Share a favorite
Halloween memory or
story about you.*

Year ____

_____
_____
_____
_____
_____
_____

Year ____

_____
_____
_____
_____
_____
_____

Year ____

_____
_____
_____
_____
_____
_____

November 1

Complete this sentence: "Three of the most important people in my life are _____."
What are some ways these people add value to your life?

Year ___

_____

_____

_____

_____

_____

_____

Year ___

_____

_____

_____

_____

_____

_____

Year ___

_____

_____

_____

_____

_____

_____

November 2

Superman is archenemies with Lex Luthor.
Batman faces off with the Joker. Do you have a nemesis?
If so, who is it, and what puts the two of you at odds?

Year ____

_____
_____
_____
_____
_____
_____

Year ____

_____
_____
_____
_____
_____
_____

Year ____

_____
_____
_____
_____
_____
_____

November 3

Charles Kettering said, "Believe and act as if it were impossible to fail." If you knew success was inevitable today, what big goal would you pursue?

Year ____

_____
_____
_____
_____
_____
_____

Year ____

_____
_____
_____
_____
_____
_____

Year ____

_____
_____
_____
_____
_____
_____

November 4

Quick, name three
reasons it is good
to be you.

Year ____

_____

_____

_____

_____

_____

_____

Year ____

_____

_____

_____

_____

_____

_____

Year ____

_____

_____

_____

_____

_____

_____

November 5

Henry Thoreau said, "I am grateful for what I
am and have. My Thanksgiving is perpetual."
What are you thankful for today?

Year ____

_____
_____
_____
_____
_____
_____
_____

Year ____

_____
_____
_____
_____
_____
_____

Year ____

_____
_____
_____
_____
_____
_____

November 6

Marthe Troly-Curtin said, "Time you enjoy wasting
is not wasted time." Describe how you
would happily waste away an ideal weekend.

Year ____

_____
_____
_____
_____
_____
_____

Year ____

_____
_____
_____
_____
_____
_____

Year ____

_____
_____
_____
_____
_____
_____

November 7

What blessings (big or small)
are you are especially thankful for
at home?

Year____

_____
_____
_____
_____
_____
_____
_____

Year____

_____
_____
_____
_____
_____
_____
_____

Year____

_____
_____
_____
_____
_____
_____

November 8

What blessings (big or small)
are you are especially thankful for
at work?

Year____

_____
_____
_____
_____
_____
_____
_____

Year____

_____
_____
_____
_____
_____
_____
_____

Year____

_____
_____
_____
_____
_____
_____

November 9

Describe a recent
adventure that you
are especially grateful for.

Year____

_____
_____
_____
_____
_____
_____

Year____

_____
_____
_____
_____
_____
_____

Year____

_____
_____
_____
_____
_____
_____

November 10

*Why do you think
so many people are unappreciative
of what they have?*

Year ____

_____
_____
_____
_____
_____
_____

Year ____

_____
_____
_____
_____
_____
_____

Year ____

_____
_____
_____
_____
_____
_____

November 11

*Name a teacher, coach, or mentor you
are especially thankful for, and share
a valuable lesson you learned from this person.*

Year____

_____

_____

_____

_____

_____

_____

Year____

_____

_____

_____

_____

_____

_____

Year____

_____

_____

_____

_____

_____

_____

November 12

Sam Lefkowitz said, "When asked if my cup is half-full or half-empty my only response is that I am thankful I have a cup."
How would you answer this question about your cup?

Year ____

_____
_____
_____
_____
_____
_____

Year ____

_____
_____
_____
_____
_____
_____

Year ____

_____
_____
_____
_____
_____
_____

November 13

Psalm 136:1 says, "Give thanks to the Lord for he is good."
What ways has God shown you goodness recently?
List at least three evidences of His goodness.

Year____

_____
_____
_____
_____
_____
_____
_____

Year____

_____
_____
_____
_____
_____
_____
_____

Year____

_____
_____
_____
_____
_____
_____

November 14

*Has it been easy or difficult for you
to be grateful over the last month?
Explain your answer.*

Year ____

_____
_____
_____
_____
_____
_____

Year ____

_____
_____
_____
_____
_____
_____

Year ____

_____
_____
_____
_____
_____
_____

November 15

Who do you sometimes take for granted?
How would you like to better express your
gratitude to this person in the future?

Year ____

_____

_____

_____

_____

_____

_____

Year ____

_____

_____

_____

_____

_____

_____

Year ____

_____

_____

_____

_____

_____

November 16

If a friend or family member saw
you acting ungrateful,
what would you want them to do?

Year ____

_____
_____
_____
_____
_____
_____

Year ____

_____
_____
_____
_____
_____
_____

Year ____

_____
_____
_____
_____
_____
_____

November 17

*What Thanksgiving tradition
are you most looking forward to,
and what makes this ritual so meaningful?*

Year____

_____

_____

_____

_____

_____

_____

Year____

_____

_____

_____

_____

_____

_____

Year____

_____

_____

_____

_____

_____

_____

November 18

Describe a favorite Thanksgiving memory
from childhood. Then explain why this time
was so meaningful to you.

Year ____

_____

_____

_____

_____

_____

_____

Year ____

_____

_____

_____

_____

_____

_____

Year ____

_____

_____

_____

_____

_____

_____

November 19

*Do you think it is easier for
a rich person or a poor person
to be grateful, and why?*

Year ____

_____
_____
_____
_____
_____
_____

Year ____

_____
_____
_____
_____
_____
_____

Year ____

_____
_____
_____
_____
_____
_____

November 20

Imagine that you have a life-threatening illness,
and you only have a month left to live.
What people or things will you be most thankful for, and why?

Year ____

_____
_____
_____
_____
_____
_____

Year ____

_____
_____
_____
_____
_____
_____

Year ____

_____
_____
_____
_____
_____
_____

November 21

Do you consider yourself
a grateful person?
Why or why not?

Year ____

_____

_____

_____

_____

_____

_____

Year ____

_____

_____

_____

_____

_____

_____

Year ____

_____

_____

_____

_____

_____

_____

November 22

Who do you need to thank?
What did this person do for you,
and how will you express your appreciation?

Year ____

_____
_____
_____
_____
_____
_____

Year ____

_____
_____
_____
_____
_____
_____

Year ____

_____
_____
_____
_____
_____
_____

November 23

*What is your favorite
Thanksgiving dessert, and when is
the last time you indulged in it?*

Year ___

_____

_____

_____

_____

_____

_____

Year ___

_____

_____

_____

_____

_____

_____

Year ___

_____

_____

_____

_____

_____

_____

November 24

Arnold Schwarzenegger says, "Pain makes me grow.
Growing is what I want. Therefore, for me, pain is pleasure."
What trial can you look back on with gratitude?

Year ___

_____

_____

_____

_____

_____

_____

Year ___

_____

_____

_____

_____

_____

Year ___

_____

_____

_____

_____

_____

November 25

What is your favorite Thanksgiving side dish?
Ideally, how often would you indulge
in this preferred entree?

Year ___

_____
_____
_____
_____
_____
_____

Year ___

_____
_____
_____
_____
_____
_____

Year ___

_____
_____
_____
_____
_____
_____

November 26

*Zig Ziglar says, "The more you express gratitude
for what you have, the more likely you will have even more
to express gratitude for." What are you thankful for today?*

Year ___

_____

_____

_____

_____

_____

_____

Year ___

_____

_____

_____

_____

_____

_____

Year ___

_____

_____

_____

_____

_____

_____

November 27

Whose life have you brightened this year,
and how are you a blessing
to this person?

Year ____

_____

_____

_____

_____

_____

_____

Year ____

_____

_____

_____

_____

_____

_____

Year ____

_____

_____

_____

_____

_____

_____

November 28

*Tell a story about something
generous someone did
for you this year.*

Year _____

_____
_____
_____
_____
_____
_____

Year _____

_____
_____
_____
_____
_____
_____

Year _____

_____
_____
_____
_____
_____
_____

November 29

Tell a story about
something kind you did
for someone else this year.

Year____

_____
_____
_____
_____
_____
_____
_____

Year____

_____
_____
_____
_____
_____
_____
_____

Year____

_____
_____
_____
_____
_____
_____
_____

November 30

Holiday decorations seem to go up earlier and earlier.
In your opinion, do the Christmas festivities start too soon,
at just the right time, or not fast enough?

Year ____

_____
_____
_____
_____
_____
_____

Year ____

_____
_____
_____
_____
_____

Year ____

_____
_____
_____
_____
_____

December 1

According to the song "Santa Claus is Comin' to Town,"
Santa keeps a list of who is naughty and who is nice.
Why should Santa put you on the nice list this year?

Year ____

_____
_____
_____
_____
_____
_____

Year ____

_____
_____
_____
_____
_____
_____

Year ____

_____
_____
_____
_____
_____
_____

December 2

Imagine waking up on Christmas Day and finding coal in your stocking.
You realize Santa placed you on the naughty list.
Tell a true story that explains why.

Year ____

_____

_____

_____

_____

_____

_____

Year ____

_____

_____

_____

_____

_____

_____

Year ____

_____

_____

_____

_____

_____

_____

December 3

If you could spend this Christmas in any part of the world.
Where would you go, what would you do,
and who would you take with you?

*Year*____

_____

_____

_____

_____

_____

_____

*Year*____

_____

_____

_____

_____

_____

_____

*Year*____

_____

_____

_____

_____

_____

_____

December 4

When is the right time to open presents?
Should they be opened on Christmas Eve,
Christmas Day, or at another time? Why?

Year ____

_____
_____
_____
_____
_____
_____

Year ____

_____
_____
_____
_____
_____
_____

Year ____

_____
_____
_____
_____
_____
_____

December 5

Do you dream of a white Christmas,
or would you rather have Christmas
be snow-free? Why?

Year ____

_____
_____
_____
_____
_____
_____

Year ____

_____
_____
_____
_____
_____
_____

Year ____

_____
_____
_____
_____
_____
_____

December 6

Imagine you are the innkeeper at the first Christmas.
Joseph and a very pregnant Mary knock on your door.
There is no room left in your inn. What will you do?

Year ____

_____
_____
_____
_____
_____
_____

Year ____

_____
_____
_____
_____
_____
_____

Year ____

_____
_____
_____
_____
_____
_____

December 7

What will you and your family
do to celebrate the birth of Christ
this holiday season?

*Year*___

_____
_____
_____
_____
_____
_____

*Year*___

_____
_____
_____
_____
_____
_____

*Year*___

_____
_____
_____
_____
_____
_____

December 8

The Christmas season can be stressful.
What is the main contributor to your
holiday stress this year?

Year ____

_____
_____
_____
_____
_____
_____

Year ____

_____
_____
_____
_____
_____
_____

Year ____

_____
_____
_____
_____
_____
_____

December 9

Imagine a Christmas fairy offers to grant you one wish.
The only rule is you cannot wish for more wishes.
What will your request be?

*Year*____

_____

_____

_____

_____

_____

_____

*Year*____

_____

_____

_____

_____

_____

_____

*Year*____

_____

_____

_____

_____

_____

_____

December 10

The Christmas season
can be an incredible time of joy.
Describe something that lifts your holiday spirits.

Year ____

_____
_____
_____
_____
_____
_____

Year ____

_____
_____
_____
_____
_____

Year ____

_____
_____
_____
_____
_____

December 11

What have you done recently to act like a Grinch?
If you could travel back in time and change how you behaved,
what would you do differently?

Year ____

_____
_____
_____
_____
_____
_____

Year ____

_____
_____
_____
_____
_____
_____

Year ____

_____
_____
_____
_____
_____
_____

December 12

Do any family members frustrate you over the holidays?
If so, what will you do to be a peacemaker
when tensions run high?

Year____

_____
_____
_____
_____
_____
_____

Year____

_____
_____
_____
_____
_____
_____

Year____

_____
_____
_____
_____
_____
_____

December 13

*Imagine a master chef offers to prepare
your Christmas dinner Describe the perfect
Christmas meal you will have him cook.*

Year ____

_____
_____
_____
_____
_____
_____

Year ____

_____
_____
_____
_____
_____
_____

Year ____

_____
_____
_____
_____
_____
_____

December 14

*In Matthew 5:44, Jesus exhorts His followers to love
their enemies. What will you do to love someone you
don't especially like over this Christmas season?*

Year____

_____
_____
_____
_____
_____
_____
_____

Year____

_____
_____
_____
_____
_____
_____
_____

Year____

_____
_____
_____
_____
_____
_____

December 15

If you knew you would only
receive one Christmas gift this year,
what would you want it to be?

*Year*____

_____

_____

_____

_____

_____

_____

*Year*____

_____

_____

_____

_____

_____

_____

*Year*____

_____

_____

_____

_____

_____

_____

December 16

Do you think electronic devices such as smartphones, computers,
and videogames distract you from the joy of the season?
If so, how will you manage them better?

Year ____

_____

_____

_____

_____

_____

_____

Year ____

_____

_____

_____

_____

_____

_____

Year ____

_____

_____

_____

_____

_____

_____

December 17

*What is
the best gift that
you have ever received?*

*Year*____

_____

_____

_____

_____

_____

_____

*Year*____

_____

_____

_____

_____

_____

_____

*Year*____

_____

_____

_____

_____

_____

_____

December 18

Imagine Santa loans you his sleigh
and flying reindeer for twenty-four hours.
Where will you go, and what will you do?

Year ____

_____
_____
_____
_____
_____
_____

Year ____

_____
_____
_____
_____
_____
_____

Year ____

_____
_____
_____
_____
_____
_____

December 19

*If you woke up tomorrow
and found your yard covered in snow,
what would you do first?*

Year ___

_____
_____
_____
_____
_____
_____

Year ___

_____
_____
_____
_____
_____
_____

Year ___

_____
_____
_____
_____
_____
_____

December 20

*Norman Peale said, "Christmas waves a magic wand over this world,
and behold, everything is softer and more beautiful."
What beautiful things are happening in your life?*

Year ____

_____
_____
_____
_____
_____
_____

Year ____

_____
_____
_____
_____
_____
_____

Year ____

_____
_____
_____
_____
_____
_____

December 21

*What are some of your
favorite things
about winter?*

Year ____

_____

_____

_____

_____

_____

_____

Year ____

_____

_____

_____

_____

_____

_____

Year ____

_____

_____

_____

_____

_____

_____

December 22

Imagine you wake up on Christmas Day, like Cindy Lou Who,
and find no presents underneath your tree.
What will you do to celebrate Christmas anyway?

Year ____

_____
_____
_____
_____
_____
_____

Year ____

_____
_____
_____
_____
_____
_____

Year ____

_____
_____
_____
_____
_____
_____

December 23

*If Frosty the Snowman suddenly showed up
at your house, how would the two of you
spend the day?*

Year ___

_____
_____
_____
_____
_____
_____

Year ___

_____
_____
_____
_____
_____
_____

Year ___

_____
_____
_____
_____
_____
_____

December 24

Describe a Christmas present
that brought you joy.
What did you like about this gift?

Year ____

_____
_____
_____
_____
_____
_____

Year ____

_____
_____
_____
_____
_____
_____

Year ____

_____
_____
_____
_____
_____

December 25

It's Christmas Day.
What three things
are you grateful for?

Year ___

_____
_____
_____
_____
_____
_____

Year ___

_____
_____
_____
_____
_____
_____

Year ___

_____
_____
_____
_____
_____
_____

December 26

No two snowflakes are exactly alike.
No two people are the same, either.
What makes you unique?

Year ____

_____
_____
_____
_____
_____
_____

Year ____

_____
_____
_____
_____
_____
_____

Year ____

_____
_____
_____
_____
_____
_____

December 27

*What do you consider to be
one of your hottest moments
with your spouse?*

*Year*___

_____

_____

_____

_____

_____

_____

*Year*___

_____

_____

_____

_____

_____

_____

*Year*___

_____

_____

_____

_____

_____

_____

December 28

When your spouse brags about you,
what would you like
your spouse to share?

Year _____

_____

_____

_____

_____

_____

_____

Year _____

_____

_____

_____

_____

_____

_____

Year _____

_____

_____

_____

_____

_____

_____

December 29

*What grand gesture
of love would you
most appreciate?*

Year ____

_____

_____

_____

_____

_____

_____

Year ____

_____

_____

_____

_____

_____

_____

Year ____

_____

_____

_____

_____

_____

_____

December 30

What actions could your spouse take to
turn a mediocre connection into
a "hot" moment?

Year ____

_____
_____
_____
_____
_____
_____

Year ____

_____
_____
_____
_____
_____
_____

Year ____

_____
_____
_____
_____
_____
_____

December 31

Looking over the past year, what is one
of your favorite memories, and what made
this experience so meaningful to you?

Year____

_____

_____

_____

_____

_____

_____

Year____

_____

_____

_____

_____

_____

_____

Year____

_____

_____

_____

_____

_____

_____

Closing Reflections

Congratulations on reaching the end of this journal. Hopefully you feel more connected to your loved one than ever before and have developed a powerful connection habit. To conclude this journey here is a final set of questions to ask your spouse that will help you evaluate your experience.

- What did you enjoy most about completing this journal together?
- What are some new insights you gained about me?
- What did you learn about yourself?
- How was it helpful to have a daily journal and connection routine?
- Now that the two of us have reached the end of this journal, how will we continue to connect?

One option for ongoing connection is to repeat the questions in this journal for up to two more years. Simply add in your new answers in the spaces provided on each page. Challenge yourselves to dive deeper into each other's inner worlds by give a different answer each year.

You might also decide to take a break for journaling for a time and replace it with another simple connection habit such as walking, chatting about your day, or enjoying coffee together. Whatever you decide, I wish you many joyful connection moments in the years ahead!

End Notes

1. Johnson SM, Moser MB, Beckes L, Smith A, Dalgleish T, et al. *Soothing the Threatened Brain: Leveraging Contact Comfort with Emotionally Focused Therapy*. PLOS ONE 8(11): November 2013. e79314. doi:10.1371/journal.pone.0079314

2. Keynes Maynard John, *Economic Possibilities for our Grandchildren,* Essays in Persuasion, New York: W.W.Norton & Co., 1963, pp. 358-373.

3. Eisenberger, I Naomi, et al. *Does Rejection Hurt? An fMRI Study of Social Exclusion*, Science Volume 302, October 10, 2003.

4. Gadoua Pease Susan, *Are You Among the Growing Number of Unhappy Married People?*, Psychology Today, Posted Sep 27, 2017. https://www.psychologytoday.com/us/blog/contemplating-divorce/201709/are-you-among-the-growing-number-unhappy-married-people

Thumbs Up
or Thumbs Down

Thank you for purchasing this book!

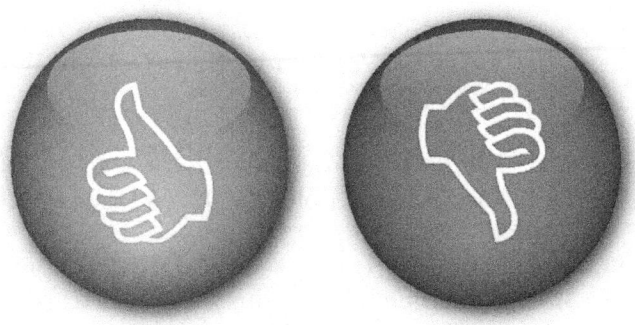

I would love to hear from you! Your feedback not only helps me grow as a writer, but it also helps me to get books into the hands of those who need them most. Online reviews are one of the biggest ways that independent authors like me connect with new readers.

If you loved the book, could you please share your experience? Leaving feedback is as easy as answering any of these questions:

- What did you like about the book?
- What is your most important takeaway or insight?
- What have you done differently—or what will you do differently because of what you have read?
- Whom would you recommend this book to?

Of course, I am looking for honest reviews. So if you have a minute to share your experience, good or bad, please consider leaving a review!

I look forward to hearing from you!

Sincerely,

COFFEE SHOP CONVERSATIONS

About the Author

Jed Jurchenko is a husband to an amazing wife, a father to four incredible girls, and a foster-father to two more. He is also a psychology professor, therapist, and author of over twenty books. Jed helps busy couples, families, and entrepreneurs grow their relationships by focusing their attention on the ones who matter most.

Jed graduated from Southern California Seminary with a Master of Divinity and returned to complete a second master's degree in psychology. In their free time, Jed and Jenny enjoy walking on the beach, reading, and spending time together as a family.

Continue the Conversation

If you enjoyed this book, I would love it if you would leave an honest review. Your feedback is a huge encouragement to me as an emerging author and helps books like this one get noticed. It only takes a minute, and every review is greatly appreciated. Oh — and please feel free to stay in touch too.

Email: jed@coffeeshopconversations.com
Twitter: **@jjurchenko**
Website: www.coffeeshopconversations.com

More Creative Conversations

This book and other creative conversation starters
by Jed are available at www.Amazon.com.

Transform your relationship from dull and bland to inspired, passionate, and connected as you grow your insights into your spouse's inner world! Whether you are newly dating or nearing your golden anniversary, these questions are for you. This book will help you share your heart and dive into your partner's inner world.

131 Creative Conversations for Couples

More Creative Conversations

These creative conversation starters will inspire your kids to pause their electronics, grow their social skills, and develop lifelong relationships!

This book is for children and tweens who desire to build face-to-face connections and for everyone who wants to help their kids connect in an increasingly disconnected world. Get your kids talking with this activity book the entire family will enjoy.

131 Conversations That Engage Kids

Made in United States
North Haven, CT
21 November 2021

11323878R00212